Old
Berkshire
Tales

Old Berkshire Tales

Cecilia Millson

With illustrations by Don Osmond

COUNTRYSIDE BOOKS

COUNTRYSIDE BOOKS
3 CATHERINE ROAD,
NEWBURY, BERKSHIRE

ISBN 0 9095392 69 8

Produced through MRM (Print Consultants) Ltd., Reading
Typeset by Acorn Bookwork, Salisbury
Printed in England by J. W. Arrowsmith Ltd., Bristol

Acknowledgements

Nine years have passed since the publication of my first book of Berkshire stories and it was with great pleasure that I accepted Nicholas Battle's invitation to write *Old Berkshire Tales*. During those nine years I have enjoyed a happy association with Countryside Books over stories of several counties.

I would like to thank all who have helped me in my research for this book with special thanks to Reg. Morris who arranged my visit to the Royal Holloway College, to Judith Hunter for information concerning Richard, Earl of Cornwall's connection with Cippenham, and Daphne Phillips for help with the story of the Castle Inn at Salt Hill.

As always the staffs of the Reading and Newbury Libraries, and the *Newbury Weekly News* have been most kind, and I would like to acknowledge with thanks the information obtained from the pages of that paper and from those of *The Reading Mercury* and *The Berkshire Chronicle*.

Finally, a special thank you must go to Don Osmond, whose lively and observant illustrations have added sparkle both to this and to other books of Tales in the series which sprang from that first one of nine years ago.

Contents

The
Eccentric Baronet
of Windsor

MANY MEN have gone to great lengths to win rich wives but
few can claim such a record as Sir John Dineley-
Goodere, the Poor Knight of Windsor. This great eccentric
was the second son of Samuel Goodere of Monmouthshire.
Samuel, captain of the man-of-war *Ruby*, had an elder brother,
a baronet, Sir John Dineley-Goodere of Burhope in Welling-
ton, Herefordshire. No love existed between the two brothers,
and as their relationship deteriorated the baronet, who had no
surviving children, announced that he intended to disinherit
Samuel in favour of a nephew, John Foote of Truro, Cornwall.
This was too much for Samuel who immediately planned to
stop such an outrageous act.

Before the baronet had time to put his threat into action
Captain Goodere arranged for him to be kidnapped in Bristol.
He was then taken aboard the *Ruby* where he was murdered
by two sailors on the night of Sunday, 18th January, 1740.
However the crime was discovered; Samuel Goodere and his
two accomplices were hanged at Bristol the following April.

Thus Edward, Samuel's eldest son, inherited his uncle's
title and estates, but when he died insane in March, 1761, at
the age of thirty two, they passed to his younger brother, John.

The new baronet lost little time in disposing of what
remained of the family fortune and he was forced to sell

Burhope in 1770. Fortunately he had some influential friends who procured for him the pension and residence of a Poor Knight of Windsor although he hardly fulfilled the original requirements for members of that Order. They were elderly soldiers of gentle birth who were appointed to St George's Chapel, Windsor, by Edward III in 1348 to pray for the Sovereign and the Garter Knights. (Since 1833 they have been known as the Military Knights of Windsor and are selected on account of their distinguished military service to be the local representatives of the Knights of the Garter at services in St George's Chapel.)

Not surprisingly Sir John discarded the disgraced name of Goodere and from then onwards was known only by the name of Dineley. However, he had no intention of fading into obscurity. Quite the reverse, for he made sure that he was noticed as he went about the historic town.

His eccentric behaviour and conspicuous style of dress made him the talk of Windsor. He left his securely locked house, to which no-one was admitted, very early in the morning to purchase his meagre provisions. His dress was of the period of thirty years before. A large cloak, called a requelaure, was worn over an embroidered coat, a silk flowered waistcoat and faded velvet breeches. His thin legs were encased in a dirty pair of silk stockings. Dingy silver buckles adorned his half polished shoes, and pattens were worn if the streets were muddy. A formidable umbrella was carried as a further precaution against inclement weather, and a cocked hat and scantily powdered wig completed his day-to-day attire. For more important outings he wore a gold laced hat (the lace was rather tarnished) and a freshly powdered best wig.

One obsession now dominated Sir John's life. This was the dream of influential family connections of ancient origin, and the wealth that would be his if he could establish the authenticity of his claim. However, to do this he needed money. As far as he could see there was only one way of obtaining this elusive commodity and that was by making an advantageous

10

marriage. It all seemed so simple to him. Surely some rich woman would like to be married to a baronet even if her affection for him personally was but slight?

His strange appearance attracted many side-long glances from the ladies. Sir John was quick to distinguish the derisive from those of more sober interest. He disregarded any giggling females but approached, with great dignity, any lady whom he deemed worthy of his attention.

In his capacious pockets Sir John carried many leaflets, printed in his own hand, which set out his marriage proposals. Some were embellished by a suitable verse of romantic poetry. With a most courtly bow he approached the chosen lady and presented her with a copy of his proposal so that she might study it at her leisure.

It was not only in Windsor that he looked for a bride. Two or three times a year he would visit London and place advertisements in the fashionable daily papers so that the ladies would know when he intended to visit Vauxhall or the theatres. He was convinced that they would flock to meet him, and he was not entirely disappointed. Curiosity is a wonderful incentive – but there the interest ceased. The honour of marrying Sir John Dineley did not tempt any lady to part with the money he required for such matrimonial bliss.

Lack of success did not daunt him. He persisted in his quest. Everything was planned on a sound commercial basis. He even had a sliding scale. The younger the lady, the less he demanded. However, he needed at least one hundred pounds to start his research so that was the lowest figure – for a lady of under twenty one years. For a lady of more advanced age the fee was higher but whoever accepted his hand might one day share his fortune. This tempting offer fell on deaf ears.

Sir John persevered quite seriously until the end of his life, but without success. He died a batchelor in 1809 at the age of eighty years, and was buried in St George's Chapel. At his death the baronetcy became extinct and the Poor Knight's claim to family fame and fortune remained but a dream.

The Excursion

A CLOUDLESS SKY dawned over the village of Bucklebury-cum-Marlston on a Saturday morning in July, 1910, and seventy two happy and excited people tumbled from their beds. It was the day of the annual choir outing. They were going to the seaside. Choir members from the churches of both parishes, together with their families and friends, were to be the guests of two Reading businessmen who resided in the locality, The Right Honourable G. W. Palmer at Marlston House, and Mr. A. W. Sutton at Bucklebury Place.

The special train to the coast was to leave Midgham station at 7 am. After an early start and a journey to the station by brake, the happy party was on its way. The ladies were jubilant. An uncomfortable night, with hair twisted in paper curlers, was worthwhile now that the resultant curls were so attractive. Summer dresses, carefully starched and ironed, and beribboned hats, firmly pinned in place against the expected sea breezes, were all that could be desired. It was only natural that some questions were asked in lowered tones, 'Had Mrs. — worn that hat last year, and had it now been refurbished with new ribbons and roses?' 'How did Mrs. — manage to dress herself and her young daughters so well on the meagre wages of her husband?'. Had the inquisitive ladies but known the truth, the last of those dresses had been finished in the early hours of the morning while the children were asleep, dreaming of the delights which the day would bring to them. Chief of these would be their first glimpse of the sea, for summer holidays were few and far between in those days and this annual outing was precious to both parents and children.

The men, although wearing their Sunday best, were not so fashion conscious. Those who had enjoyed past excursions gave the benefit of their experience to the newcomers and told them what they might expect on arrival at the Isle of Wight, their ultimate destination.

Those who were fortunate enough to obtain window seats on the train were the envy of others who were tightly packed into the middle of the carriages, but the more kindly souls offered to change about as the train sped through the Hampshire countryside.

Portsmouth was reached at 9.50 am and the party dispersed to pursue their own amusements until lunchtime. Some chose to explore the dockyard and visit H.M.S. *Victory*, others strolled along the front towards Southsea. The Vicar, the Rev. Edward Thorp, accompanied by those whom he described in the next month's parish magazine as 'being the more nautical members of the party' boarded the *Duchess of Fyfe* for a trip round the Isle of Wight.

All was well until the Needles loomed in sight. The calm sea and gentle breeze had encouraged the party to stay on deck to watch the sportive porpoises and the sea birds but suddenly all was changed. The sea became rough and the breeze stiffened and most of those nautical members disappeared below decks. Only the more resilient were left to enjoy a good view of the Needles. Fortunately there were calmer waters ahead. By the time Ryde was reached at 4 pm all were ready for tea.

The remainder of the party had lunched at the Speedwell Hotel at Portsmouth before crossing on the ferry to Ryde and were waiting there to greet them. These excursionists spent a pleasant afternoon on the beach where the children paddled and built sand castles under the watchful eye of the organist and choirmistress. As she was also a teacher at the village school few would deny that she was quite capable of deterring any youngsters who might feel inclined to wander away on their own devices.

As it happened it was not the children who got lost. The return train was due to leave Portsmouth at 7.45 pm and it did so promptly. The vicar and fifteen of the party could vouch for

that for they arrived at the station just in time to see it disappearing into the distance!

It seemed probable that they might have to stay overnight. But help was at hand. It so happened that the chairmakers of Wycombe had chosen that same day for their annual outing.

The 'Wycombe Chairmakers' Excursion' train was stand-

ing in the station, and the organisers kindly agreed to take the vicar and his companions on board. There were sighs of relief. At least the stranded party would arrive somewhere nearer home. After recovering from the first shock, plans to catch up with the rest of their party were discussed and formulated. They decided to throw a note on to the platform as the train passed through Winchester station begging that contact be made with the Reading station-master asking for the Midgham train to be halted there for a time. The next step was to see the station master at Basingstoke when the Wycombe train stopped there. He was asked to use his influence so that the Wycombe train could make a brief unscheduled halt at Reading to allow the errant party to alight. Agreement was reached. As the train came to a halt at Reading, the vicar marshalled his companions and with more haste than dignity they leapt from the train during its momentary pause. To their immense relief they found that the message they had thrown from the train at Winchester had achieved the desired result. The Midgham train was waiting in the station, and they were reunited with their families.

No doubt the talk of their adventures occupied the remainder of the journey from Reading to Midgham where the brakes were waiting to take them to their respective churches. As they walked from there to their homes in the moonlight everyone agreed it had been a wonderful and exciting day out at the seaside.

Ladye Place

OF ALL THE manors granted by William the Conqueror to Geoffrey de Mandeville the Thames-side manor of Hurley was surely one of the most beautiful.

It was a perfect site for the Priory which his second wife Lasceline persuaded him to build both as an act of thanksgiving for the vast territories which the king had bestowed upon him, and as a tribute to the memory of his first wife, Athelaise. The priory was to become a cell of the Abbey of Westminster where she was buried.

Today, the parish church of St Mary the Virgin, once the Priory church, stands as a reminder of that ancient foundation, together with the dovecote, the great tithe barn (now a private house) and the monastic fishponds. The Benedictines lived and farmed at Hurley for over four hundred and fifty years before the Priory was suppressed with other lesser monastaries in 1536.

It must have been a forlorn group of monks who left their peaceful home to travel to Westminster. They took with them their copy of the foundation grant of the Priory, and other deeds, and deposited them at the Abbey where they remain to this day.

In 1540 it was the turn of the Abbey of Westminster itself to surrender its possessions to King Henry VIII and a year later the manor of Hurley was granted by the monarch to Charles Howard. In 1543 he sold the property to Leonard Chamberlayn for the sum of £116 plus 850 marks. His ownership was brief and he conveyed the manor to John Lovelace in 1545.

The new owner built himself a Tudor mansion in the

precincts of the Priory, over the burial crypt of the monks. The choice of the site seems odd but these underground vaults were destined to play a part in the nation's history during the 17th century.

John Lovelace called his new house 'Ladye Place' in honour of the Virgin Mary to whom the Priory had been dedicated. His grandson, Richard Lovelace, was evidently a man of adventure. He sailed with Sir Francis Drake, and from his share of the treasures seized from captured Spanish galleons, he was able to improve and embellish the house which he inherited from his father in 1601. Richard Lovelace, who also served in the Irish wars, was knighted in Dublin in 1599, and was created Lord Lovelace of Hurley by Charles I in 1627.

It was his grandson John, the third Lord Lovelace, who brought notoriety to Ladye Place. An ardent Whig, he was arrested in 1683 for alleged conspiracy in the Rye House Plot whereby it was planned to seize King Charles II and James, Duke of York, at Rye House in Hertfordshire as they returned from Newmarket. The Whigs had hoped to compel the King to summon Parliament but the plot failed. Some of the ring-leaders were executed, others were imprisoned. Lovelace was freed but continued his subversive activities. After the death of Charles II he was among those who wished to see James II deposed in favour of his eldest daughter Mary and her husband, William, Prince of Orange.

Lord Lovelace entertained lavishly at Ladye Place and under the cover of this hospitality a chosen few of his guests would pass quietly through a secret entrance to the crypt. In the eerie surroundings of that ancient place the conspirators discussed their hopes for the deposition of James, but Lovelace again came under suspicion and was imprisoned by order of the King in 1688. He was released when James fled from the country and William and Mary accepted the crown of England.

Lovelace was rewarded for the part he had played in the 'Glorious Revolution' when he was made Captain of the Gentlemen Pensioners by William III. The King also honoured Ladye Place with a visit so that he could see for himself where the conspirators had held their secret meetings on his behalf.

Extensive alterations and interior decorations to the house were carried out by Lord Lovelace. Continued extravagant entertainment also helped to deplete his financial resources. At his death in 1693 his cousin, another John Lovelace, inherited an estate encumbered by debts, and the manor was sold by decree of the Court of Chancery so that the creditors could be paid.

The days of the Lovelaces of Hurley were over. The house passed through several hands in the ensuing years but enjoyed another day of glory on the 14th November 1785, when King George III and Queen Charlotte were entertained at Ladye Place.

It was a brief respite. In 1837 the house was demolished after the last tenant moved away. He was Gustavus Adolphus Kempenfelt, whose brother Admiral Kempenfelt went down in the ill-fated *Royal George* on the 29th August 1792. No buyer could be found for the historic mansion which was not altogether surprising. Not only had it become dilapidated through the neglect of its later owners but even when in good repair it had certain disadvantages. A report of 1794 stated that while the downstairs salons were spacious and decorated in the Italian style, the 'upper rooms were small and the gutters of the roof ran through them, freely admitting both water and air.' Evidently the 19th century house purchasers were looking for properties which could provide greater comfort than that offered at Ladye Place. Or it may have been that the discovery of the bodies of three monks, still clad in fragments of their black habits, underneath the floor of the crypt frightened away prospective buyers!

A new Ladye Place has now replaced the Tudor mansion of John Lovelace, but the Benedictines who were forced to leave their riverside haven so many centuries ago have left several interesting reminders of their long tenure to enhance the natural beauty of the Hurley of today.

The
Hungerford Murders

W HEN PC WILLIAM GOLDBY left Hungerford Police Station at ten o'clock on December 11th 1876 to start his night duty he little realised that it would be a patrol that he would never forget.

It was not a pleasant evening. The winter sky was heavy with clouds which promised rain before morning but the dimly lit streets were quiet enough. The constable looked forward to the normal round of routine calls as he walked the familiar beat. He expected to meet up with Inspector Joseph Drewett on the outskirts of the town but as there was no sign of his superior, the constable took a turn along the road leading to Wantage. He knew that the Inspector was due to meet PC Thomas Shorter at the Folly crossroads, less than a mile north of Hungerford, shortly before 10 pm. By now he should be down Eddington hill past the tollgate and quite close at hand.

PC Goldby was not unduly worried when the Inspector failed to appear. It was more than probable that he had gone in pursuit of poachers. There were many in this area and members of the constabulary were always on the alert for signs of their presence. PC Goldby continued his trudge up the hill, glancing from time to time into the dense woods which bordered both sides of the road. He was pleased to reach the top where the trees thinned a little and the light was better.

Then a dark form, sprawled across the road, brought him to an abrupt halt.

At first the constable thought he had found a drunken man, but when he approached the prostrate figure he was horrified to find that it was the body of PC Shorter, his head so battered that he was scarcely recognisable. The attacker must have worked swiftly. The dead man's truncheon had not been drawn.

The shocked policeman ran back to the tollkeeper's house. He told the keeper and his wife to watch for any who passed that way and then went on to Hungerford to raise the alarm. When he reached the police station and told his fearful news a messenger was immediately sent to Superintendent Bennett at Newbury. PC Goldby then returned to the scene of the crime accompanied by PC Charles Brown.

Inspector Drewett was still unaccounted for and the two men were fearful for his safety. The threatened rain started to fall to add to their discomfort as they hurried up the hill. Upon arrival at the crossroads they parted company. PC Brown took the right hand lane while Goldby searched the one to the left. A startled call from his colleague sent him hurrying across to the place where Brown stood, some twenty yards from the turnpike road. Together they gazed down in horror at the body of Joseph Drewett. His face was blackened by a gunshot wound which had penetrated his neck at close range. Also, he had been battered about the head and, like his subordinate, he had not drawn his truncheon in self defence. The attack had been swift and savage. Under the body was a cloth cap.

Supt. Bennett had lost no time in driving to Hungerford from Newbury in his pony and trap, accompanied by two of his men, and immediately commenced his investigations. The turnpike keeper and his wife reported that they had seen William Day and his son-in-law, William Tidbury, returning to Hungerford by the turnpike road. The inspector was interested. Both men were known to be notorious poachers. Furthermore, Tidbury had two younger brothers, Henry and Francis, who were well known to the gamekeepers. The cap

21

was inspected and considered to be similar to one worn by Henry Tidbury.

The evidence was slight but sufficient for Supt. Bennett to take action. William Day was arrested as he sat at breakfast in his cottage at Eddington. His son-in-law who lived at the same address had left for work but was soon apprehended at a nearby farm as he tended the threshing machine. His brothers were taken in for questioning from the local foundry where they worked as strikers. By 9 am all four suspects were in custody.

In vain did Day protest that on the previous evening he was repairing a threshing machine at Lower Hidden Farm, assisted by William Tidbury. He said that they finished work around 10.30 pm and then walked down the hill together to Eddington. Yes, he said, he had noticed a figure in the road but, thinking it was a drunken man, had taken no further notice of him.

William Tidbury stated that he had gone to bed about 8.30 pm but on being told that he had been seen much later by the tollkeeper he said that he had made a mistake – of course, he had helped his father-in-law at the farm. It was not convincing evidence.

Henry and Francis Tidbury proved truculent witnesses and refused to answer questions. In all the conduct of the four men did nothing to allay suspicion.

During the day the chief constable of Berkshire came in person to take charge of the investigation. He called upon a skilled moulder from the foundry to make wax impressions of footprints found at the scene of the crime. They were found to be identical with impressions made by boots worn by the Tidburys. Another find, a trigger plate from a sporting gun, was considered part of a dismantled gun found hidden near the Tidbury's cottage. This evidence was sufficient to convince the Coroner's inquest that the four men were guilty of the murders and they were held in custody to await trial at the next assizes.

While they waited, the funeral of the murdered policemen

took place at Eddington Church. It was attended by the two widows, and four of the five children of Inspector Drewett, the chief constables of Berkshire and Wiltshire, and many colleagues and friends. Six police superintendents acted as pall bearers and bore the coffins to adjacent graves in the country churchyard. In Hungerford the shops were closed and the blinds drawn as the whole town mourned the loss of two gallant men. A subscription fund was opened for the widows and fatherless children. Donations were generous, especially when it was realised that Mrs. Shorter would receive no gratuity. Her husband had served for just over two years but a service of three years was required before the widow became

23

eligible for a gratuity. The worthy people of Hungerford put their hands deeply into their pockets to help the bereaved woman.

In February 1877 the four accused men stood in the court at Reading before Mr. Justice Lindley. The evidence which had been collected was formidable. The distinctive patterned cap, the footprints, the hidden guns, the fact that all four men had been seen walking up Eddington hill on that fateful evening, and two had been seen making the return journey – but that was where the counsel for William Day challenged the evidence. Was it likely, he said, that a guilty man would walk down a turnpike road and expose himself to public view?

William Tidbury admitted that he had made a false statement to the police but when all the evidence had come to light it appeared that he had tried to shield his brothers who had admitted their guilt to him when, on hearing the gunshots, he had gone to investigate and had come upon the scene of the murders. Henry and Francis put up little defence, and PC Brown gave evidence that Henry had recently admitted to him that it was he who had shot the Inspector.

The outcome of the trial was that Day and William Tidbury were acquitted but Henry and Francis were found guilty and the death sentence was passed upon them. It was carried out at Reading gaol on Monday March 12th 1877, the first time that an execution had taken place inside the prison. Until then all such hangings had been witnessed by the public but on this occasion only the chaplain, a doctor, and members of the press were present. About 500 people gathered outside the prison but as the black flag was hoisted they dispersed quietly.

The public, however, still wanted information about the last chapter in this sad story and local papers were in great demand, especially when it became known that the convicted men had confessed to the crime before their deaths.

The Newbury Weekly News printed a special Monday issue of 7,500 copies many of which were despatched to Hungerford. The newspaper shop was so besieged with customers that a policeman was called to keep order.

Henry and Francis Tidbury confessed that they had been challenged by the policemen as they were poaching pheasants on that December night. Francis was arrested but Henry, instead of escaping, stayed to help his brother. After a brief struggle the Inspector was shot. Another shot was aimed at PC Shorter who, as he turned to go for assistance, was pursued and struck down in the road. Henry then went back to retrieve his cap and found that the Inspector was still alive. The unfortunate man was kicked and beaten by the brothers until he was seen to be dead. In the confusion the cap was forgotten.

Two wayside crosses still mark the places where the policemen fell, sombre reminders of a tragedy which shocked Hungerford and the whole of Berkshire on that ill-fated night over one hundred years ago.

Francis Cherry
The
Jacobite Squire

F RANCIS CHERRY, a delightful name for a man, who from all
accounts personified the best qualities of an English country squire. He cared for his tenantry, entertained lavishly, was
a superb horseman, a good scholar, and a sincere friend.
Shottesbrooke was indeed fortunate in its lord of the manor at
the end of the seventeenth and beginning of the eighteenth
centuries. No doubt the villagers fully appreciated their good
luck in that Francis Cherry differed greatly from his father, the
unpopular William Cherry, whom Thomas Hearne mentioned in his diary of 1731 as being 'father of, but of very
different principles from my best friend, Mr. Francis Cherry'.

Born around the year 1665, Francis Cherry grew into a
handsome young man. He became a gentleman commoner of
Edmund's Hall, Oxford, and when only twenty years of age
married Eliza Finch of Fiennes Court, White Waltham. The
young couple lived with William Cherry until his death in
1689, when he left debts for them to settle amounting to
£30,000. Francis Cherry undertook to pay these in full
although by so doing he was placed in severe financial straits.
Eventually, thank goodness, his finances recovered. However,
a matter of conscience was to mar his complete happiness for
the remainder of his life.

Having taken an oath of allegiance to King James II, he could not bring himself to transfer his loyalty to the King's daughter and her Dutch husband when they succeeded to the deposed king's throne following the Glorious Revolution of 1688. King William III and Queen Mary II found no favour with Mr. Cherry. He became a determined Jacobite.

The manor house at Shottesbrooke, which could accommodate as many as seventy guests, became a refuge for those of the same principles. These included Bishop Ken, Robert Nelson, who mentioned his kind host in his *Memoirs of the Pious Robert Nelson*, and Henry Dodwell, a noted scholar of Roman history. He had been forced to relinquish his Oxford professorship because he, too, had refused to take the oath of allegiance to William and Mary.

It was Francis Cherry and Henry Dodwell who first recognised the outstanding abilities of young Thomas Hearne, the son of White Waltham's parish clerk. George Hearne taught his son to read and write but poverty forced him to send the boy to work during the day. Fortunately he came to the notice of the squire who virtually adopted him and sent him to school at Bray. The boy's aptitude for learning astonished his masters and Cherry entered him at Edmund Hall, Oxford in 1695 – paying all his expenses. He was rewarded by knowing that his protegé did well at the University. Hearne became second librarian at the Bodleian and would have attained even higher distinctions but that he followed the lead of his benefactor and remained an ardent Jacobite. His preferment at Oxford was doomed when he refused to take the oath of allegiance to George I in 1715, but he quietly continued with his historical and literary works until the end of his life.

Before that era Francis Cherry had done his best to change the course of history. So devoted was he to the Stuart cause that he was prepared to lure King William III to his death. It was well known that the King was jealous of Cherry's prowess in the hunting field and hated to be outshone by the hard riding squire. One day, when hunting in the Windsor area, Cherry realised that he was closely followed by the King. Here was a chance to rid England of the Dutch usurper! Without hesitation Cherry rode his horse into a deep and dangerous part of the Thames. He hoped that William would follow and fail to negotiate the hazardous course. The ruse failed. For once the King was willing to give way to Cherry's superiority in the saddle. He turned away his horse and remained unharmed. It was left for a mole, at a later date, to succeed where the squire had failed.

When William met his death in 1702 as a result of his horse's unfortunate tumble over a mole hill, he was succeeded by his sister-in-law, the Princess Anne. Francis Cherry resolutely refused to recognise Queen Anne, just as he had refused to accept the sovereignty of her late sister and brother-in-law. However, being a perfect gentleman he had no wish to embarrass any lady. When hunting in the precincts of Windsor Forest he contrived to avoid the royal party when the Queen chose to follow the hunt in her chaise. The Queen reciprocated by respecting his principles. She once described her unwilling subject as 'the most honestest gentleman in my dominions' and even directed her steward to send him presents of red and white wine from the royal cellars as a neighbourly gesture.

Squire Cherry died on September 23rd 1713 and it was found that he had left instructions that his funeral should be simple and take place at 10 pm. In accordance with these wishes four of his tenants carried him the short distance from his home to his grave in Shottesbrooke churchyard two days later. A plain black marble slab inscribed with the year of his death and the epitaph 'Hic jacet peccatorum maximus' (Here lies the chief of sinners) was laid over the resting place of this most respected English gentleman.

Molly Mogg, the Beauty of Wokingham

WHEN THE early 18th century landlord of the Rose Inn at Ockingham (Wokingham) welcomed a party of diners to his inn he little thought that by their pens, his daughter's name would become a household word, not only in Berkshire but far beyond the county's borders.

John Mogg knew his customers well. Alexander Pope lived at Binfield and would frequently call at the inn with his friends, Dean Swift, John Gay, and Dr. Arbuthnot, but on this particular occasion they stayed longer than usual, detained by a violent storm.

To while away the time they wrote verses to Molly, one of the landlord's two beautiful daughters. John Gay is thought to have been the chief author of the ballad but Pope and Swift probably contributed some of the lines. Dr. Arbuthnot seems to be a doubtful collaborator as some versions of the story do not acknowledge his presence on that afternoon.

The first verse introduces the love-sick admirer and names the cause of his dejection:

> Says my Uncle, I pray you discover
> What hath been the cause of your woes
> Why you pine and whine like a lover?
> I've seen Molly Mog of the Rose.

29

The next thirteen verses sing her praises and tell of the young man's obsession with his love. To quote but one:

> A letter when I am inditing
> Comes Cupid and gives me a jog,
> And I fill all the paper with writing
> Of nothing but sweet Molly Mog.

The final verse tells of his consuming jealousy and the apparent hopelessness of his suit:

> While she smiles on each guest like her liquor
> Then jealousy sets me agog,
> To be sure she's a bit for the Vicar,
> And so I shall lose Molly Mog.

One can imagine the laughter and sallies as the verses were composed by gentlemen who had dined and wined well at the old inn.

There was obviously scant sympathy for the forlorn young man. He is thought to be Edward Standen of Arborfield, the last male heir of the manor which had been held by his family since 1589. He died in 1730 at the age of 27.

The ballad first appeared in *Mist's Weekly Journal* under the title 'Molly Mog, or the Fair Maid of the Inn.' It was noted 'that it was writ by two or three men of wit, upon the occasion of their lying at a certain Inn at Ockingham, where the daughter of the House was remarkably pretty, and whose name was Molly Mog.' (*Oxford Companion of English Literature.* 1940.)

The fair lady's name also figured in a Welsh ballad:

> 'Some sing Molly Mogg of the Rose
> And call her the Ockingham belle
> Whilst others does ferses compose
> On beautiful Molly Lapelle.'

31

One wonders if the young lady in question became embarrassed by the publicity, but undoubtedly it was good for business as it attracted customers to the inn. Molly's sister was reputed to be even more attractive and it has been suggested that the ballad referred to Sarah, or Sally, and not to her elder sister. But Alexander Pope would have known the landlord's daughters well and would have been unlikely to confuse the two sisters.

In spite of her beauty Molly Mogg remained a spinster to the end of her days. She outlived her parents and her brother and sister. She died at the age of 67 on Sunday, March 9th 1766. The record of her death describes her as 'Mrs. Mary Mogg, advanced in years but in her youth a celebrated beauty and toast, possessed of a good fortune that she has left among her relations.'

Apparently her brother had two daughters and no son so that on the death of Mary, or Molly, Mogg the family name died with her. It was a strange name but one made famous as those noted wits toyed with words on a stormy afternoon.

From a
Country Churchyard

CHURCHYARD MEMORIALS provide an interesting study for those who care to browse round 'God's acre'. Were the departed really as virtuous as their relatives would have us believe, or were the sentimental verses chosen from a book thoughtfully provided by the monumental masons? This frequently occurred but, no doubt, some epitaphs were specially composed to do honour to the deceased or to tell the story of their demise.

The workmates of Henry West were obviously shocked and distressed when the young man was killed while working at Reading railway station in 1840, and with genuine grief erected a monument over his grave in the churchyard of St Lawrence's Church.

IN MEMORY OF HENRY WEST
Who lost his life in a WHIRLWIND at the
GREAT WESTERN RAILWAY STATION, READING
on the 24th. of March, 1840 – Aged 24 Years.
Sudden the change. I in a moment fell
and had not time to bid my friends farewell
Yet hushed be all complaint, tis sweet, tis blest,
to change Earth's stormy scenes for Endless Rest.
Dear friends prepare, take warning by my fall,
so shall you hear with joy your Saviour's call.

The wooden monument or 'rail' which marks his grave has been renewed three times, in 1862 by his brother George, in 1924 by his niece F. G. Rixon, and in 1971 by the Reading Corporation. It stands by the footpath leading from the Forbury to Blagrave Street, and serves as a reminder of the terror which swept through Reading on that Tuesday afternoon as well as a memorial to the unfortunate young man who was struck down so suddenly.

The *Reading Mercury* reported 'the whole neighbourhood of Friar Street was alarmed by a loud noise resembling the crashing of heavy timber or the rolling of thunder. This noise was found to have originated at the Station.' Apparently a violent gust of wind struck the railway station where several men were erecting a large shed next to the station house 'to provide for the comfort of passengers'. Although others were injured, Henry West was the only fatal casualty. He was working on the lantern, a large wooden structure on top of the building which was to provide light for the waiting room. Although it weighed four tons it was carried over the station house by the force of the wind. It damaged a chimney and then fell to the ground. Henry West was found two hundred yards away. He was carried to the Boar's Head in Friar Street but death had been instantaneous.

A wooden memorial of the same 'rail' design can be found near the church of St Mary the Virgin in Bucklebury village. It was erected in the 19th Century to the memory of John Crook. Its message is brief and to the point:

> Cease dear friends and weep no more
> I am not lost but gone before.
> Dear friends all, where'er you be
> Prepare yourselves to follow me.

A monument in another country churchyard was designed with considerable thought for the future. It was erected in 1855 to commemorate Job Lousley of the Manor House, Hampstead Norreys, whose generosity to his dependants made him a well loved lord of the manor. Not only is the monument itself unusual but the story behind its erection must be unique.

Job Lousley had expressed a wish to be buried on his own land in Beech Wood. Hurried consultation took place with the Bishop of Oxford but permission was refused for the use of this unorthodox site and Job Lousley was laid to rest in the churchyard in July 1855. When it was decided to erect a large monument over his grave his tenantry participated in a most practical manner.

The wives of his tenant farmers and farmworkers gathered together broken ploughshares and pieces of other farm implements. So anxious were they to help to show their regard for a man who had been helpful to them that they were able to send two cartloads of metal to Bucklebury foundry. After it was melted down it was used to erect a cast iron monument. It rises tier by tier, rather like a huge wedding cake, and is surmounted by an obelisk. As members of the Lousley family have joined their ancestor in the family tomb their names have been added on panels which are fixed to the sides of the tiers.

The last name is that of Conrad Offa Lousley who died on November 9th 1962. He was the ninth and last surviving child of Luke, eldest son of Job Lousley. After a long career in India he retired to Bradfield in Berkshire and at his death was taken back to his native village for burial with his family.

In spite of being unable to comply with his father's last wish, Luke Lousley did his best to make amends. He placed a granite memorial on the place in Beech Wood where his father used to stand to gaze over the manorial lands which he farmed and loved so well.

There is a memorial to a vastly different type of man in the churchyard of St Michael and All Angels at Lambourn. It tells its own story:

Here
lies the body
of JOHN CARTER
of this parish, labourer,

> who in the defiance of the laws
> of God and man
> wilfully and maliciously
> set fire in two places
> to this town of Lambourn
> on the 19th day of November 1832
> and was executed at Reading
> in the 30th. year of his age
> on the 16th. day of March, 1833
> having desired that his body
> might be interred here as a
> warning to his companions
> and others who may hereafter
> read this memorial to his
> untimely end.
> The wages of sin is death.
> Repent and turn yourselves from
> all your transgressions and so iniquity
> shall not be your ruin.

One wonders if John Carter did truly express the wish that such a memorial should be erected, or whether it was the outcome of a pious hope of those responsible for its erection that the wording might deter others from committing such a futile act of folly.

An eighteenth century monument in the churchyard of All Saints, Wokingham, provides ample space for the recording of family history. Benjamin Beaver used a large rectangular block of Portland stone to mark the graves of his wife, Elizabeth, and their nephew, Thomas Leach. On one side is inscribed:

> Erected for the lasting remembrance of one
> of the best women who deserved more than
> I can say of her and for whose sake I have engaged
> part of my estate to keep up this monument in
> repair to the end of time.

36

A suitable verse extolling her many virtues accompanies this inscription.

Also recorded is a tragic event which grieved both Mr. and Mrs. Beaver some twenty six years before her death.

> Stop youth. Take warning for here lieth also
> the remains of their beloved nephew Thomas Leach
> who was lost July 14th 1761 in swimming
> in the river Thames, near Caversham Lock, to the great
> sorrow of all who knew him. In the 16th year of his age.

With these two epitaphs one side of the monument was complete. But in order to fill the remaining three sides Benjamin Beaver then set about the task of recording the family history from the time of Charles I.

The misfortunes caused by the Civil War took pride of place. A certain Richard Beaver was a loyal supporter of King Charles and, at his own expense, raised and trained a troop of horse to serve his royal master. His brother-in-law, Sir Richard Harrison of Hurst, raised two troops, and together they joined with other friends in the neighbourhood to fight beside the King. They suffered heavily for this loyalty. It is recorded that Richard Beaver, Alexander Troughton and the family of the deceased Algernon Sime, suffered persecution and the sequestration of their estates and goods by Parliament.

Alexander Troughton's son-in-law, Thomas Bowden, also paid a high price for serving his sovereign. He was a coal merchant who supplied the court at Windsor. One can imagine the amount of fuel needed to give some semblance of warmth in that great castle. With the defeat of the King the bills were not paid and it is stated that 'he lost his Debt of Thousands by the unfortunate King being destroyed'.

Another story related by Mr. Beaver is that of Henry Dean, a cousin of Lady Harrison. Apparently this unfortunate man was forced to earn his living as a publican after lending money to John Hawes, a brewer of Wokingham. The money was never repaid. As if this was not enough, Dean's involvement in the Civil War reduced his income still further until he had nothing left but a tenement of £3 a year. At fifty years of age he became a gardener, a hard life for a man 'not being used to work'. He followed this occupation until he was eighty years of age. It is a comfort to know that in spite of these misfortunes Henry Dean remained 'patient, healthy, and of a cheerful and honest heart'. He died at the age of eighty five. Obviously he had thrived on hard work but Benjamin Beaver added a warning note:

'Let this deter others lest they ruin themselves and their families as Algernon, Alexander, and the said Richard did theirs.'

Lastly an epitaph which says much about the trials of an eighteenth century coachman in a very few words. It is inscribed upon the tomb of James Murray in Speen church-yard. Many coaches travelled through that village on their way from London to Bath and the coachman had no easy task to drive the heavy vehicles along the rutted roads in all weathers, to please their passengers, to be on the alert for possible attacks from highwaymen, and satisy their employers and innkeepers by keeping to the scheduled timetables. It was a long hard road and for one the end of the journey appears to have been a welcome release from his trials and tribulations.

In memory of
James Murray
Late Bath Coachman
who died 20th May, 1796
Aged 46 years.
Tho' while on earth I did remain
I was reproach and scorn by men
But now am numbered with the saints
And saf'd of all my long complaints.

Berkshire Fairs

EAST OR MARKET ILSLEY
AN IMPORTANT
TRADING CENTRE SINCE THE 13th CENTURY
WAS GRANTED A ROYAL CHARTER IN 1620.
ON THIS SITE WERE HELD THE SHEEP FAIRS
WHICH IN IMPORTANCE WERE SECOND ONLY
TO SMITHFIELD AND WERE HELD FORTNIGHTLY
FROM APRIL TO OCTOBER.
THE LAST ONE WAS HELD IN 1934.

THIS INSCRIPTION on a wayside plaque in the centre of East Ilsley is a reminder of the times when the village was thronged with sheep and its twenty four inns and public houses were frequented by the farmers, drovers, and shepherds, who came to the fortnightly sales.

Since prehistoric times men have travelled the Berkshire Downs, and ancient tracks lead down to this village which was a trading centre even before it became famous for its sheep fairs.

The charter of 1620, granted by James I, gave royal approval to the great sheep fair held at the end of July or beginning of August. This continued to be the most important of the many fairs held in East Ilsley. As many as 80,000 sheep were penned in the village on one occasion during the 19th century. Throughout the year an average sale was around 400,000 sheep. The pens lined the sides of the street and trees were planted to provide shade for the animals as they waited patiently for the highest bidders to become their new owners.

The noise and bustle must have been tremendous at the fortnightly sales when men, sheep and dogs thronged the roads. In between the fairs East Ilsley retained its unusual appearance with the empty pens standing row upon row along the village street but these short breaks must have given the inhabitants welcome spells of peace – except, perhaps, the landlords of the inns!

Cosburn's directory of 1901 lists eighteen fairs at East Ilsley during that year, of which March 27th was a fair for both sheep and cattle, April 10th, the Easter fair, May 29th the Whitsun Fair, and October 13th the hiring fair. At this last, shepherds, farm hands and servants changed their employment, if they so wished, for the coming year.

J. E. Vincent, writing in the *Highways and Byways of Berkshire* at the beginning of the century, gave a word of warning to cyclists, and the few motorists of those days, who were likely to visit East Ilsley. He wrote of the chalk and flint roads leading to the village from Steventon in the north, or from Compton to the east. Although normally not bad roads, when the flocks of sheep had passed over them the surface was destroyed and the little flints were churned up to stand as sharp as swords, to the detriment of tyres. Mr. Vincent had evidently needed to mend a puncture when he travelled the byways to the fair. It was the introduction of modern transport which finally caused the decline of the sheep sales. The drovers no longer had to walk their animals to the country markets. Fortunately, sheep still graze peacefully on the Berkshire Downs, watched over by their faithful shepherds.

There is a lovely tale of days gone by. When a shepherd died a piece of sheep's wool would be placed in his coffin as proof of his calling. He could then convince St Peter that there was good reason for his irregular church attendance. At times his sheep needed him even on the Sabbath day, and as a good shepherd he could never neglect his flock.

It was the woollen trade which brought prosperity to Newbury, not by the sale of sheep, but in the making of their wool into fine cloth, and Newbury, too, had its ancient fairs.

The first fair was granted on the 7th July, 1215, by King John so that provision could be made for the St Bartholomew's Hospital, or almshouses, which he had founded. Appropriately, the fair was held on the day and morrow of the feast of St Bartholomew, Apostle and Martyr. (24th August).

Later, Edward IV granted two four-day fairs, one on the eve and feast of Corpus Christi and two days following, and the other on the eve and feast of the Nativity of St John the Baptist and two days following. The townspeople did not like these rather lengthy fairs when they lost their trade to the beneficiary of the fair. The profits from these two fairs were shared, two thirds going to the crown and the other third to the King's 'trusty and beloved servant, Thomas Herbert, the elder,' in recognition of his 'good, gratuitous, and laudable service'. Unfortunately, it is not known what Thomas Herbert did to receive such a favour from the King.

When Queen Elizabeth I granted the Charter of Incorporation to the Borough of Newbury in 1596, four fairs were granted annually, on the day of the Annunciation (25th March) on the Nativity of St John the Baptist (24th June) on St Bartholomew's day (24th August) and St Simon's and St Jude's day (28th October). These fairs were entitled to their own courts of Pie Powder, derived from *Pieds Poudreux* – the court of the travellers (or men with dusty feet) whereby justice could be administered on the spot to prevent any delay in the settlement of a transaction, or before the traveller went on his way. These fairs seem to have prospered judging by the increase in their profits and tolls. Newbury, on the crossroads from London to Bath and from Southampton to the North, was a good place to trade and the fairs became widely known and used for the sale and the purchase of cattle, cheese, and other commodities.

Around 1687 the Mayor and Corporation of Newbury fell into trouble by changing the venue of the fair of St Simon and St Jude from the town site to one on Wash Common on the outskirts of Newbury. The townspeople complained to the King, and the mayor, Francis Cox, was summoned before

James II and his Privy Council to explain the reason for the move with the result that he was ordered to return the fair to its original venue, although he was granted permission to hold a sheep fair separately on the common land known as West Fields.

The origin of another fair, the Statute or Michaelmas Fair, is obscure. As a Statute Fair it was probably granted by statute or ordinance of the Corporation as lords of the manor and not by royal grant or licence (*History of Newbury* by Walter Money). This would date its origin sometime after 1627, the year in which the corporation became the lords of the manor of Newbury. It is known that it was in existence before 1752 as an official announcement was made regarding a slight change of date for the Hiring Fair due to the change in the Calendar.

It became a very popular fair and one in which those seeking employment made their way to the Market Place or the Wharf, where the fair was held, and displayed an emblem of their calling. A shepherd would wear a piece of sheep's wool, a carter a length of whipcord, a cowman a piece of cowhair while a cook would carry a spoon and a maid a small mop. A prospective employer would thus distinguish the type of servant he needed and try to strike a bargain of employment for the coming year. If there was any difficulty about the signing of the bond by an illiterate man or woman, a cross would do, or, alternatively, the acceptance of a shilling by the servant sealed the agreement.

In 1893 the Newbury Corporation took steps to abolish the hiring fair. A change of attitude towards the method by which servants were engaged was making the practice of hiring at fairs unacceptable. However, there was so much opposition from some sections of the community that it was decided to hold a postal ballot to decide the matter. The result showed that most people agreed with the Corporation but, at the same time, they wanted the fair to continue as an amusement fair.

While the four ancient Newbury fairs gradually fell into disuse, the Michaelmas fair grew in popularity but its growth did cause problems in the streets, especially as the traffic increased year by year. In 1945 it was decided that the time had come to move it to Northcroft, an open space near the town, and there it is still held, as well attended as ever. The Mayor opens the fair and invites the children to join in the initial free rides. They scramble with enthusiasm on the gigantic, brightly lit, amusements – a far cry from the simple attractions provided by the showmen with the 'dusty feet'.

Reading's first fair was granted by Henry I to the Abbey which he founded in the town in 1121. He gave the Abbot and Convent the right to hold the fair on the feast of St Laurence (August 10th) and the three days following.

His grandson, Henry II, added another favour, the grant of a fair on the feast of St James (25 July) and the three days following, and stated that his 'fair peace was to protect those at the fair and those going to and returning from it'. A warning to those who might be displeased at this further grant to the Abbey at the local traders' expense, as well as to any who might be tempted to try highway robbery on the merchants who did business at the fair.

In 1206 yet another fair was granted to the Abbey by King John, a frequent visitor to Reading. This was to be on the vigil and feast of St Philip and St James (1st May) and the three days following so that thirteen days of tolls, profits, and fines from these important and lucrative fairs provided revenue for the Abbey.

By 1315 the weekly market which had been held from time immemorial at a certain place, probably St Mary Butts, was moved nearer the Abbey gates by order of the Abbot. This caused the burgesses to complain to the King, Edward II, but notwithstanding an order to the sheriff to look into the matter, the market continued to be held in the area which eventually became known as the Market Place.

However, there was some consolation for the town traders. The fair around St Laurence's feast fell into disuse and had disappeared before the middle of the 15th century. The other two fairs continued to do well and were favourite venues for

43

the settlement of debts. It was essential that this should be done when witnesses were at hand as a written record of such a transaction was rare in the days when few people could read or write, and a professional scribe was not always available.

With the Dissolution of the Monasteries the tolls and profits of the two fairs were given to Sir William Penyson but later transferred to the Duke of Somerset when his nephew, Edward VI, granted him the manor, borough and fairs of Reading. When the Duke fell into disgrace the gift was forfeited to the Crown.

On September 23rd 1560, Queen Elizabeth I granted Reading a new charter to restore the then decayed town to prosperity. In addition to the two existing fairs, the corporation was given permission to hold two more four day fairs, one on the feast of St Matthew (21st September) and the other on the Purification of the Blessed Virgin Mary (2nd February). All had their own courts of Pie Powder.

The four fairs were still being held in the 19th century although justice was administered through the normal channels by that time. Certain rules were drawn up for behaviour at fairs and markets, including one against drunkenness and disorderly behaviour.

Early in the 19th century John Howard Hinton, a Baptist minister, used the Forbury Cheese Fair to speak in favour of total abstinence. He was the first man in Reading to speak out in public on the matter, a brave action as some who frequented the fairs were not noted for sobriety and could have well shown resentment at his remarks.

Trade was brisk at these fairs. Those held in February, May, and July, dealt mainly in the sale of horses, cattle, and pigs and the one in July became so successful that it had to be transferred from sites in Broad Street and Friar Street to the open space of the Forbury in 1840.

The Michaelmas Fair was held there already. Cattle and horses were sold at this fair but originally it was used mainly for the sale of hops, serges, and cheese. During the 18th century it became one of the most important cheese fairs in the country and attracted producers from Somerset, Gloucester, Wiltshire, and Dorset. The highest quantity recorded at the fair was in 1795 when 1,200 tons of cheese were pitched for sale in the Forbury. Waggons which had delivered the cheese were laden with birch brooms which were sold in the towns on the homeward journey.

It was the opening of the Great Western Railway in 1840 which heralded the decline of this prosperous fair. When the produce was brought by rail rather than by road or the canal, the cheeses were not unloaded but left in the station while samples only were taken to the fair. The cheeses were then sold direct from the railway station.

The Michaelmas Fair was also a hiring fair and, as at Newbury, there were many seeking employment who displayed the tokens of their trade.

In addition to the main sales, stalls laden with household commodities, trinkets, and country produce tempted the housewives to buy while their husbands dealt with the major purchases.

It was not all business. The fairs provided plenty of amusements and people were in holiday mood. Peepshows, booths, swings and roundabouts were packed into any available space, and cheap-jacks and gipsies peddled their wares. Wombwell's menagerie was one of the chief attractions but those who participated in the business or fun of the fair needed to be wary, as the Earl of Abingdon's steward found to his cost in 1814. He had been given £240 with which to buy grey horses but a pick-pocket relieved him of the money before he had made his purchase. Human nature had not changed since the days when Henry II granted his 'fair peace' to protect those who went to Reading fair.

Although the market continues, the days of the great fairs has passed but in their time they contributed both to the prosperity and pleasure of many people and those who had enjoyed them never regretted that they had obeyed the call to 'Come to the Fair!'

45

Shottesbrooke Church

'Shottesbrooke Church is near Shottesbrooke Hall
The house rather great and the Church rather small.'
The Berkshire Book of Song, Rhyme, and Steeple Chime,
Arthur Humphrey, 1935

SMALL IT may be but the Church of St John the Baptist at
Shottesbrooke is perfect in all its proportions and has been
described as a miniature Salisbury Cathedral. It is cruciform
in shape and from the centre rises a slender spire which towers
above the tall trees of Shottesbrooke Park in which the church
stands, near the manor house. It dates from the 14th century
but is thought to stand on the site of an earlier church. The
story of its origin is fascinating.

The lord of the manor, Sir William Trussell was addicted to
strong drink. After a particularly heavy session in 1337 it was
feared that he had gone too far and would surely die as the
result of his excesses. However, he managed to survive by
drinking 'water drenches and water stypes, water gruel and
water soups'. His wife was so grateful for his recovery that she
persuaded him to build a church as an act of thanksgiving as
related in the old ballad:

'An oath he sware
To his lady fair
"By the cross on my shield

46

A church I'll build"
And therefore the deuce a form
Is so fit as the cruciform,
And the Patron Saint that I find the aptest
Is that holiest water-saint, John the Baptist.'
Berkshire Book of Song, Rhyme and Steeple Chime

The new church was all but finished and only the weathervane needed to be placed on the top of the spire. However this resulted in a tragedy which must have marred the joy of the first services to be held in the church. The local smith climbed the tall spire and when his work was completed he called for a pot of ale so that he could drink the health of the king. A loyal sentiment indeed, but as the smith raised the pot to his lips he overbalanced and fell all the way to the ground. He was fatally injured of course and his grave was dug on the place where he had fallen. It was the first burial in the churchyard. A flat tombstone was placed over his grave and was inscribed with two 'O's, the last words which the poor man uttered as he fell to his death.

Sir William Trussell also founded a college in the manor for 'a warden, five chaplains, and two clerks, to celebrate mass daily for his own, and the King's soul, also those of their ancestors and descendants, and endowed it with the advowson of the Church and the rent of 40 shillings from the manor which had been acquired from the heirs of William le Breton' (Berkshire Victoria County History Vol. III. page 165). It seems that Sir William had mended his ways and was indeed a reformed man, although his good wife appears to have been forgotten in the daily prayers! However, their tombs are together in the north transept of the church.

In the latter half of the 14th century the church and college were damaged by fire but from the existing architecture of the church it is thought that the college was the most affected and the church escaped the worst of the flames.

The college was obviously restored as it continued in use until 1547 when, together with other chantries, it was confiscated by Henry VIII and its revenues forfeited to the Crown.

One who lived through these troubled times was Thomas Noke whose brass is one of the most notable in a church which has a good share of ancient brasses. Thomas, or 'Father' Noke as he was affectionately known, is depicted in his furlined gown, with his three wives and five children. The inscription tells us that

HERE LYETH BURYD THOMAS NOKE WHO FOR
HIS GREATE AGE AND VERTUOUS LYFE WAS
REVERENCED OF ALL MEN AND COMMONLY
CALLED FATHER NOKE CREATED ESQUIRE BY
KING HENRY THE EIGHT HE WAS OF STATURE
HIGH AND COMLY AND FOR HIS EXCELLENCY
IN ARTILLERY MADE YEOMAN OF THE CROWNE
OF ENGLAND WHICH HAD IN HIS LYFE THREE
WIVES AND BY EVERY OF THEM SOME FRUITE
AND OFFSPRING AND DECEASED THE 21 DAY
OF AUGUST 1567 IN THE YEARE OF HIS AGE
87 LEAVING BEHIND HIM JULYAN HIS LASTE
WIFE TWO OF HIS BRETHREN ONE SISTER
ONE ONLY SON AND TWO DAUGHTERS LIVING.

His only son, Thomas Noke, bought the manor of Shottesbrooke from Edward de Vere, 17th Earl of Oxford. The de Veres had acquired the manor when Elizabeth Trussell, heiress to the estate, married John de Vere, the 15th Earl of Oxford sometime before 1510.

Other monuments commemorate later lords of the manor and their families, including the Cherrys and the Vansittarts who bought Shottesbrooke Park from the widow and daughters of Francis Cherry in 1716.

The church was struck by lightning on Wednesday, 20th July 1757, during a violent thunderstorm. It was feared that the spire might have to be demolished but fortunately this outstanding feature of the church was saved. Falling stones from the spire damaged the roof, some of the rafters caught fire, and there was other interior damage necessitating considerable repair work which took over a year to complete. The parishioners worshipped at White Waltham church while work was in progress and returned to their own church on Sunday 24th September 1758.

During the 19th century the Victorian architect, G. E. Street, R.A., was called upon to supervise the restoration of the church. Fortunately in spite of 18th century repairs and 19th century restorations the church of St John the Baptist is still essentially the church of its founder. Those who know and love Shottesbrooke must be grateful that Sir William Trussell recovered from his self-imposed illness and expressed his gratitude by building this lovely church.

The Legend of
Hawthorn Hill

THIS IS A tale of two men – one who shrugged away good fortune and another who grasped at opportunity and with a combination of adventure, hard work, and a fair share of good luck, found wealth in an unexpected place.

It's an old story, told in varying forms in far-flung places, but Hawthorn Hill in Berkshire can lay claim to being the true location for the legend – at least it had two necessary attributes, an ancient tumulus and a thorn tree.

The story tells of an innkeeper who kept The Woodman Inn in Hawthorn. However, he had a recurring dream in which he was advised to leave his home to travel to London Bridge where he would hear something to his advantage. Understandably, the man thought little of the message after the first dream but when it was twice repeated he felt that he should travel to London and visit London Bridge to determine whether there was any truth in the matter.

It was quite an undertaking in those far off days for there were no proper roads. The Innkeeper had probably never left his home before, and the area around Hawthorn Hill was thickly wooded. Tales of footpads would be known to the host of a wayside inn where travellers called for a night's lodging rather than face the perils of passing through unknown territory after dark. The dream must have been very convincing to make him bundle up a few belongings and set off for London on such a hazardous journey.

At that time old London Bridge was bordered by shops. The Berkshire innkeeper paused to wonder at the unfamiliar sights when he finally reached his destination. As he was pondering on his next move he was approached by a shop-keeper who enquired if he could be of help to the bewildered stranger. The countryman replied that he was a newcomer to the city, then, encouraged by the friendliness of the shop-keeper, he related his strange dream. The Londoner was amazed when he heard the tale. This man had left his inn to travel unknown paths to London, all on account of a dream! He could not help but laugh at the foolishness of this country bumpkin and advised him to return home before ill befell him in the streets of the city. Then, struck by a strange coinci-dence, he said that he too had once experienced a similar dream in which he had been told to travel to a place called Hawthorn. He had been told that on arrival at this unknown place he must look for a hill on which grew an ancient thorn tree. If he dug underneath the tree he would find a pot of gold. The shopkeeper laughed. What nonsense it all was. As if he was going to leave his shop on such a crazy errand.

Nonsense indeed agreed the innkeeper, who could hardly conceal his excitement. He thanked the London man for his good advice and said he would return home and forget the whole thing. He hurried back to Hawthorn because he knew full well where a thorn tree grew on the top of a hill, a tumulus in fact; just the place to find hidden treasure. When he reached his Inn again he grabbed a spade and rushed off to the mound. It was not easy, digging down into the hard ground but he worked away and at last his spade struck the side of a pot. The dream came true – the pot was full of gold!

Legend does not relate if the Innkeeper had a wife and family, but if he did they must have been delighted at the prospect of sharing his new-found wealth. However, their pleasure would have been shortlived. Alas, it was a case of 'easy come, easy go'. The innkeeper lived well and entertained his friends lavishly. The gold dwindled and went. Only the old pot stood on the shelf, a reminder of the prophetic dream.

One day two scholars from Oxford called at the inn for refreshment. They saw the pot and inquired if they might examine it more closely. A strange inscription round the rim had attracted their notice. The innkeeper lifted it down from the shelf and handed it to the scholars. He said that he had often wondered about the lettering but he could not decipher the inscription. His guests studied it well and gave him the translation:

> Beneath the place where this pot stood
> There is another twice as good.

The innkeeper looked at the scholars in bewildered amazement. Surely there could not be another pot! Could his luck really be this good? Once more the innkeeper took his spade to dig deeper into the mound. Once more he had the good fortune to strike the side of a pot with the spade and sure enough there was an identical pot – except for one thing, this one had no inscription. His hands trembled as he lifted it from the ground and hurried back to the inn. As the golden coins tumbled on to the table he vowed he would be a wiser man this time and handle his riches with more care. This was his final chance – the uninscribed jar told of no further treasure. He was as good as his word although he still welcomed travellers to his inn so that they could find comfort and shelter within its walls, but it was no longer called The Woodman but aptly renamed The Money Pot.

Treasures
of the
Lambourn Valley

THE LAMBOURN VALLEY has much to offer those who travel
Berkshire's highways in search of natural beauty or historic landmarks. The road follows the river as it winds
through rich pasture land, bordered by picturesque cottages,
fine racing stables, and parish churches which invite closer
inspection. They are rich in history and three in particular
possess treasures which arouse varying emotions as the visitor
looks upon them for the first time.

One evokes a feeling of amused surprise, another a touch of
nostalgia for bygone days, and the third is so perfect that the
onlooker must pause in sheer wonder at its beauty.

A collection of elephants' heads is an unexpected find in a
country church but the Rev. William Nicholson, a 19th century cleric, saw nothing incongruous in placing them along-
side the more conventional angels in St Swithun's church,
Wickham.

The old Saxon tower, which originally stood aloof from the
church, must have witnessed many arrivals at the Norman
doorway but, surely, none so strange as the three elephants'
heads which were brought by the vicar from the 1862 Paris
Exhibition.

It is rumoured that the reverend gentleman intended to

hang them in the vicarage. Alas, his wife was less than enthusiastic about the idea. In vain did her husband explain that he saw them as symbols of three Christian virtues, namely, Fortitude, Docility, and Strength. The disappointed vicar may have felt in need of these virtues himself when his protegés were turned from the door.

However, he was not to be beaten. He decided to take them to his church. They could hang in the extension which he had recently caused to be built so that the tower could be incorporated in the main building. It was an excellent idea, he felt, to relieve the bareness of the north aisle by placing the giant heads to join the angels which already adorned the nave.

The vicar was so pleased with the result that he ordered five more heads from British craftsmen. The eight trophies of his triumph over adversity still hang from the oak rafters which they appear to support. It is but an illusion. They are made of papier-mache.

A nearby church dedicated to St Andrew serves the beautiful village of Boxford where the Lambourn flows by the old mill, a scene much loved by artists. The church, although renovated many times, retains some of its treasures. A barrel organ dating from the days of George III must have brought joy to the congregation as they sang their hymns and psalms to its accompaniment, and listened to the secular tunes which would have been used for voluntaries. No doubt the country people arrived early and lingered after the service to enjoy the melodies played on their new organ. Its five barrels had a repertoire of fifty tunes in all. Sadly it is silent now, worn out by constant service, and money cannot be spared for its repair. Indeed there are many claims on people's generosity these days but one day, perhaps, the money will be found to renovate this little organ which provided the music for a parish church so many years ago.

The village of Eastbury can also claim to bring pleasure to the passer-by with its thatched cottages and old dovecot. Yet another treasure awaits those who tread the well worn path to the church of St James the Greater. The door opens to reveal a superb window 'In Celebration of the Lives of Edward Thomas, Poet, and Helen, his wife.'

Engraved by Lawrence Whistler, the window portrays two trees, one budding, one bare, which provide a framework for scenes beloved by the poet and his wife, and the symbolic hands of sunlight which gently touch their names. Lines from his poems recall the love of Edward Thomas for the English countryside and the shadows of the war which tragically claimed his life at Arras in 1917. A poignant reminder of his wartime service is the inclusion of a helmet and Sam Browne belt which hang from the winter tree.

His wife outlived him by fifty years, the last twelve of which were spent in Eastbury. Her own books *As it was* and *World Without End* are remembered in the window. Helen Thomas is buried in the peace of the country churchyard.

The idea of the memorial came from their younger daughter who taught at Lambourn School. Over six hundred people subscribed to the cost of the window which was dedicated on October 16th 1971.

As one gazes into its depths the poet's own words are recalled:

'There I find my rest, and through the dusk air
Flies what yet lives in me. Beauty is there.'

Thomas Holloway

P ATENT MEDICINES became increasingly popular during the second half of the 19th century when affluent Victorians cast aside their well tried natural remedies in favour of the fashionable new products which filled the shelves of the apothecaries' shops. In the most prominent positions one was sure to see those bearing the brand name of HOLLOWAY. The demand for Thomas Holloway's products did not entirely depend upon their efficacy but also upon their producer's ability to advertise them. Members of the public were left in no doubt at all that Holloway's ointment and pills were essential to their wellbeing.

Are you in agony? – A Well Spring of Hope for all.
HOLLOWAY'S OINTMENT.

To the very core and centre of all diseases which effect the surface of the body this remarkable preparation penetrates.

It disappears as if it were literally drawn down by some internal force and performs its healing errand, safely and without pain.

This advertisement appeared in the *Reading Mercury* during 1860. It claimed that this wonderful ointment cured a variety of complaints 'whether in the skin, the flesh, the glands, or among the muscles'. It could be obtained from 'The Establishment of Professor Holloway of 224 The Strand (near Temple Bar) London, and from all respectable druggists and dealers in medicine throughout the civilised world'.

The ointment ranged in price from 1s.1½d. to 33s. a pot but, it was pointed out, there was a considerable saving by buying the larger sizes!

During 1860 there was an outbreak of diptheria in Reading. At once another advertisement appeared which advised the townspeople to take Holloway's pills as soon as symptoms of a sore throat appeared so that the dreaded illness might be checked in its early stages. A masterful stroke of propaganda which sent the frightened populace scurrying to buy the precious pills. It was by grasping every such opportunity to promote his sales that this enterprising man succeeded in building up his very profitable business.

Thomas Holloway was born on September 22nd 1800 at Plymouth Dock (now Devonport) where his father, a retired warrant officer, had opened a baker's shop. Later the family moved to The Turk's Head Inn at Penzance, and Thomas attended school locally and at nearby Cambourne until he reached the age of sixteen. When his father died, his mother was left to provide for her numerous family, and with the help of both sons, Henry and Thomas, she ran a grocery and bakery business in the Market Place at Penzance. Thomas remained with her until he was twenty eight when he felt that it was time for him to seek better prospects in London. Soon after his arrival in the city he met Miss Jane Driver whom he eventually married. It was to prove an ideal match as his wife joined enthusiastically in her husband's ventures throughout their married life.

After various jobs, in 1836 Thomas Holloway became a merchant and foreign commerical agent, an undertaking which was to change his life. Among his clients was a native of Turin, Felix Albinolo, who had settled in London. This man prepared an ointment from a secret recipe which he called 'Albinolo's or the St. Come et St. Damien ointment'. With Thomas Holloway's assistance it was accepted for use at St Thomas's Hospital, a circumstance which set Mr. Holloway thinking that here was an opportunity to use his own skills. He considered the possibility of preparing a harmless concoction

to be known as 'Holloway's family ointment'. It was on sale by October 1837.

A year later an advertisement appeared in *Town* accompanied by a recommendation for the ointment from no less a person than Herbert Mayo, the senior surgeon of the Middlesex Hospital. Thomas Holloway was on the road to success, but there were pitfalls during the early years after he established his small warehouse in the Strand and added the sale of pills to that of his now lucrative ointment. The advertisements proved very expensive and debts threatened to overwhelm him as they had overwhelmed Felix Albinolo, but Thomas and Jane lived simply and worked hard. With his wife to help him in the preparation of his remedies Holloway, a man of good looks and persuasive charm, was free to travel both the town and country regions to sell his wares. He also visited the dock areas where he took care to interest both sailors and travellers in his products. He assured them that the pills and ointments would safeguard them from illness both during the voyage, and throughout their period abroad. In this way his preparations and the belief in their success were carried to foreign lands. Undoubtedly, some curative properties were present to give satisfaction, otherwise his customers would not have repeated their orders as they did. At length the business prospered, creditors were paid in full and Thomas and Jane Holloway began to reap the benefits of their hard work. They became immensely rich.

His warehouse in the Strand was demolished in 1867 to make way for the new Law Courts and so alternative premises were obtained in Oxford Street. Here one hundred people were employed in addition to the numerous salesmen. The proprietors lived on the premises, but as careful investments and successful speculations increased his wealth, Thomas Holloway looked for a suitable house away from London. As a result of their searchings, he and Jane moved to Tittenhurst at Sunninghill in Berkshire. Sadly his wife did not live long to enjoy her new home for she died in 1875 at the age of seventy one. There were no children of the marriage and the broken hearted widower looked for ways of spending his now vast fortune.

Surprisingly, his offer to benefit his native town was not well received by its officials, and so Thomas Holloway then sought the advice of Lord Shaftesbury who suggested that a sanatorium for the mentally afflicted would prove of great benefit. This idea was readily adopted and the building of a hospital at Virginia Water was commenced at once. It provided accommodation for two hundred and forty patients and when completed in 1885 it was opened by the Prince and Princess of Wales, later King Edward VII and Queen Alexandra.

In the meantime Thomas Holloway had conceived the idea of also erecting a ladies' college in memory of his beloved wife. In his usual businesslike manner he lost no time in translating thoughts into deeds. He purchased ninety acres of land at Mount Lee, Egham Hill, on May 8th 1876. This site, on the Berkshire/Surrey borders was to form the Holloway College estate.

The architect who was entrusted with the design of the proposed college was William Crossland. The result was an awe inspiring building embellished with ornately designed scrolls, fruit, flowers and shells on every corner and pinnacle and over every door and window. It has to be seen for the amount of work involved in it to be fully appreciated. Local bricks were used and every stage was carefully watched by the benefactor. Although so near to his home he had a bungalow built in the grounds so that he could be at hand to see the main building grow into a massive structure of one thousand rooms, with a beautifully decorated chapel, a spacious library, and an art gallery. This gallery now houses the valuable and famous art collection which Holloway bought as he travelled Europe in search of pictures for his college. Alas, he was not to see them hung upon its walls or to watch the first students enter its doors or enjoy their leisure in its spacious grounds; he died shortly before his great work was completed. He had spent over £400,000 on the land, buildings, furnishings and pictures and he left another £300,000 to complete and endow the college.

A statue of the founder and his wife was placed in one quadrangle, and in the other, one of Queen Victoria who opened the college on June 30th 1886. The room in which she was entertained remains the same to this day.

The Royal Holloway College, University of London, remained a women's college for nearly eighty years. It was only in 1965 that male undergraduates were admitted. In 1983 the college agreed to merge with Bedford College, University of London, and the new buildings are now being erected in the grounds at Egham. The new institution, to be known as the Royal Holloway and Bedford New College will have places for nearly three thousand undergraduates in the Arts, Sciences, and Music.

Thomas Holloway died at his home in December 1883. When he died he was spending £50,000 a year on his advertisements. These had been translated into several languages and his pills and ointments had acquired a world wide reputation.

After ensuring the continued welfare of his hospital and college, and providing for his faithful employees, he left the residue of his fortune to his wife's sister, Miss Mary Ann Driver. He was buried in the churchyard of St Michael's Church, Sunninghill, where a memorial chapel was later erected to the design of William Crossland.

The simple message on his churchyard memorial 'He, being dead, yet speaketh' symbolizes the work of a remarkable man whose remedies for sick bodies not only provided the money for the treatment of sick minds, but also enabled numerous women to receive a university education at a time when their status in life made it difficult for them to obtain such recognition. A fulfilment indeed of Thomas Holloway's desire to further education through a memorial to his devoted wife and partner.

Three V.C.s of Thatcham

THATCHAM CAN surely lay claim to a rare, if not unique, record for a village community. The Victoria Cross has been awarded to three of her sons, the first in the Boer War, the second in World War I, and the third in World War II. Furthermore, the last two awards were made to two brothers. The village is justifiably proud of these men and those who served with them during times of extreme danger.

Private William House of the 2nd Battalion, Royal Berkshire Regiment, returned home from South Africa in July 1902. He had been severely wounded in action but, according to the report in the *Newbury Weekly News*, he was looking wonderfully well considering all he had been through on the battlefield. He was awarded the Distinguished Conduct Medal for his bravery and Thatcham people felt proud of the young man whom they had known since his birth in 1879. He was the eldest son of Mr. and Mrs. Thomas House of Park Lane, Thatcham.

The year following his homecoming local pride was intensified by the announcement that the award of the D.C.M. had been replaced by that of the Victoria Cross. This highest award for gallantry was conferred upon Private House for his conspicuous bravery at Mosilikatse Nek, South Africa in 1900.

The 2nd Battalion which had joined a force stationed at Pretoria under the command of Sir Ian Hamilton, was moving westwards along the southern slopes of the Magliesburg range. On the northern slopes another column was marching parallel to the 2nd Battalion. In between the Boers were putting up a fierce resistance. An attempt was made by Sir Ian to force through a mountain pass so that he could make contact with the northern column. This manoeuvre resulted in a lengthy battle in the course of which a Sgt. Gibbs went forward to reconnoitre. He was shot and fell severely wounded. Without a moment's hesitation Private House ran forward in an attempt to bring him to safety. He reached the wounded man, lifted him, and managed to carry him a few yards when he, too, was hit and fell amidst intense fire. Although in great pain he called out that no one was to go to his aid as the danger was too great.

After the South African war, Private House continued his career in the Army and volunteered for service in India. He returned to England in November, 1911, and shortly afterwards was promoted to the rank of lance corporal. He was stationed at Shaft Barracks, Dover. His friends noticed that since his return from abroad he was unusually quiet and sometimes appeared to be depressed but they were quite unprepared for the terrible event which occurred at the end of February 1912. As the lance corporal was preparing to go on parade he shot himself. It was thought that the Indian climate, coupled with the effect of the two severe head wounds which he had incurred in South Africa, had affected his health and caused temporary insanity. It was indeed a tragic end to a brave man's life.

The second Victoria Cross was awarded posthumously to Second Lieutenant Alexander Buller Turner, 3rd Battalion (attached 1st) Royal Berkshire Regiment. He was the son of Major Charles Turner and Mrs. Turner of Thatcham House and grandson of Admiral Sir Alexander Buller, G.C.B.

Described in the *Newbury Weekly News* as a 'lover of life and the happiness it brought' this twenty two year old officer saved the lives of many by his outstanding bravery.

The local paper gave the following account of the award of his V.C. 'To most conspicuous bravery on September 28th

1915 at 'Fosse 8' near Vermelles. When the regimental bombers could make no headway in Slag Alley, Second Lieutenant Turner volunteered to lead a new bombing attack.

He pressed down the communication trench practically alone, throwing bombs incessantly with such dash and determination that he drove the Germans back about 150 yards without a check. His action enabled the reserves to advance with very little loss and subsequently covered the flank of his regiment in its retirement thus probably averting the loss of some hundreds of men. This gallant officer has since died of wounds received in this action.'

In fact it was just three days after the battle, on October 1st, that Lieutenant Turner died. He was buried at Cloques, France, and is commemorated by a wall plaque in Thatcham parish church.

The news of the award of the Victoria Cross was received with gratification by those who had served with the young lieutenant. They shared the opinion of one who said, 'A pluckier man I never saw. I am proud to have served under such an officer.'

When this gallant act took place, Victor, Alexander's younger brother was a fifteen year old schoolboy at Winchester. He was commissioned into the army three years later and was to prove a valued officer.

In 1942 Lieutenant Colonel Victor Buller Turner was serving with the Rifle Brigade (Prince Consort's Own) in the Western Desert. On the night of October 27th he led the men of his battalion through 4,000 yards of difficult terrain to their objective. They successfully accomplished their mission and took forty German prisoners. The Colonel then organised the captured position for all round defence. They needed it. He and his men came under continual enemy fire from 5.30 am to 7 am as ninety German tanks advanced in waves upon their isolated position. Thirty five enemy tanks were destroyed and another twenty were immobilised. Wherever the fighting was heaviest Lieutenant Colonel Turner was there encouraging his men. When he found that one 9 pounder gun was being manned by only one officer and a sergeant he stayed to act as loader and together the three men accounted for five enemy tanks being destroyed. Although wounded in the head Victor Buller Turner refused aid until the last tank was out of action. For his personal gallantry, fine leadership, and complete disregard of danger he was awarded the Victoria Cross, just twenty seven years after his elder brother had received the same honour.

The story of the third V.C. has a happier ending than those of the other two heroes. Lieutenant Colonel Victor Buller Turner lived to see the end of the Second World War. His father had died in 1926 but his mother still lived in Thatcham and he returned home to his native village. After her death he decided to leave Thatcham and live in Suffolk where he died at the age of seventy two. The Berkshire village will long remember its three courageous soldiers, and if you visit the area of the Turner home there, Thatcham House, you will find that the road around it commemorates the gallant name — Turner's Drive.

Yattendon's Brass and Copper Craft

THE EMINENT Victorian architect, Alfred Waterhouse, who numbered among his achievements the design of the one time municipal buildings and clock tower in Blagrave Street, Reading, bought the country manor of Yattendon from Thomas Awbery Howard in 1876. It was not long before he decided to design and build a new manor house, to be known as Yattendon Court, on a hilltop site west of the village.

While they were digging out the foundations for his mansion, the workmen came upon two interesting discoveries; the oak base of an ancient beacon, and a hoard of metal implements. Both finds were carefully examined and the metal artefacts were proclaimed by archaeologists to date from the late Bronze Age. They were considered to be the stock-in-trade of a bronze founder. Little did that ancient craftsman know that centuries later his workshop area would resound once again to the noise of metal workers' tools as copper and brass utensils were beaten into shape.

Around 1885 Alfred Waterhouse's wife, Elizabeth, decided to start a weekly night school for young men and boys to give them an interest during the long winter evenings. The classes were held in the laundry of the Court and the village students were offered a good choice of subjects: writing, geography, drawing, elementary astronomy, woodwork, and a rough kind of repoussé work. This last became known as the brass beating class and quickly proved to be the most popular project.

Mrs. Waterhouse designed most of the objects. Occasionally one of her family lent a hand, or she adapted a well-known design to suit her students' needs. This personal involvement, together with her considerable artistic ability, contributed greatly to the success of the class. The Yattendon brass and copper ware had an individual quality which was to prove a valuable asset when the items they made were eventually offered for sale.

Simple pentrays and doorplates were soon considered too elementary and the metal workers eagerly embarked on more complex designs. New fenders and firescreens were proudly displayed in their cottage homes. Large water jugs were also popular. These were useful in the days before running water was available for the bathtubs. As their enthusiasm grew the men took their work home to complete and it is said that the tapping hammers could be heard all around the village.

The class soon became too large for the limited space available in the laundry and was moved to the basement of the Court. It is to be hoped that the building was soundproofed for as many as thirty hammers were beating away on busy evenings.

Henry Smith, the blacksmith from the neighbouring village of Ashampstead, was called upon to help Mrs. Waterhouse make up the work, a task which she had undertaken by herself when the classes first started. Soon Harry, the blacksmith's son, joined the team and the range of products was increased. Mr. Aldridge the estate carpenter, who already supervised the wood working class, became responsible for the preparation of the metal. He cut it to size and nailed it on to the blocks of wood in readiness for the beaters.

From making commodities for their own homes the pupils graduated to supplying them for sale to the public through a village industries shop, and at various exhibitions, including that of the Home Arts and Industries Association at the Royal

Albert Hall. As the students developed into skilled craftsmen even Liberty's of Regent Street consented to sell their products.

Churches were amongst their best customers. Font ewers, candlesticks, vases, and altar crosses were commissioned, but perhaps the metal beaters' finest work was a copper and brass ambon, a combined lectern and pulpit, which was made for the Church of the Ascension at Cala in South Africa.

5,454 pieces were produced before the First World War intervened to bring to an end this thriving village industry. Sadly, the death of Mrs. Waterhouse in April 1918, dashed any hopes that it might be revived. She was the inspiration and driving force behind the project and without her leadership the men who returned from the war did not restart their evening work. Their brass beating class was but a happy memory.

With a change of ownership in 1925 the Yattendon Court of Alfred Waterhouse was demolished to make way for a new house designed in the Tudor style, but some brass and copper ware made in the basement of the original house may be found in and around Yattendon to this day. Neither has the work of the ancient bronze founder been forgotten: His hoard is carefully preserved in the Newbury Museum.

Jethro Tull

'A S TO AGRICULTURE, it was not by choice, but a sort of
necessity that I practised it' wrote Jethro Tull, a man
who turned from law to farming and eventually became
known, at least by some admirers, as 'The father of British
agriculture.'

This unwilling farmer was born in Basildon in 1674, the son
of Jethro and Dorothy Tull. His education did little to prepare
him for a life on the land. He matriculated at St John's
College, Oxford, in July 1691 and was admitted as a student
to Gray's Inn two years later. Although he was called to the
Bar in 1699 his ambition was to enter Parliament rather than
to practise law. He was also an accomplished musician and
not only played the organ but understood its structure, something which was to influence his later achievements.

Tull was newly married to Susanna Smith, of Burton
Dussett in Warwickshire, and had settled in London when he
was prevailed upon to return to the family estates, partly due
to the death of his father and partly on account of his own
health which was causing concern. He first farmed at Howberry, near Wallingford, and at once looked for ways of
improving his land.

The theories of the 'Gentleman farmer from London' were
not well received by his farmhands. Disputes arose about the
best way to sow sainfoin (a fodder plant) with the result that
Tull used his technical knowledge gleaned from his study of an
organ's mechanism to good account. In 1701 he successfully
invented a seed drill to do the work for him. His labourers

looked askance at a machine which replaced the age-old methods of sowing used by their forefathers and the relationship between them and their employer became somewhat strained.

A move was made from Howberry to Prosperous Farm between Hungerford and Shalbourne in 1709. Tull strongly refuted suggestions that his farming methods had failed at Howberry and stated that it was purely on account of his health that he had moved to a new area.

It was to improve his failing health that he travelled on the Continent between 1711 and 1714 but he did not neglect his farming interests. On the contrary, he observed the methods used in France and Italy and was particularly impressed by the way in which the soil was pulverised between the rows of vines in the grape-growing districts. This pulverisation obviated the need to manure the soil.

When Tull returned to England he devised machinery for breaking up the soil and started to experiment on his own farm. He achieved success first with crops of potatoes and turnips and then with wheat. He thought that air, earth, and water were all that were needed for the growth of successful crops and to prove his theory grew wheat on the same field for thirteen years without the help of any fertilising agent.

Tull published his findings in *Horse-hoing Husbandry* in 1731 and followed on with *Horse-hoing Husbandry or an Essay on the Principles of Tillage and Vegetation* two years later. He was bitterly disappointed by the derision with which both publications were received in some quarters of the farming community. His ideas were ahead of his time. No doubt he made mistakes, but many of his theories were proved right by future generations, particularly those on the cultivation of potatoes, turnips, beans, and cabbages.

One man evidently appreciated his writings. When Jethro Tull died at Prosperous Farm in 1741 he was taken to his native village for burial. The Rev. George Bellas, the Rector of Basildon, noted in the church register 'Mem: This Jethro Tull, Esq. was the author of a valuable book on agriculture entitled *Horse Husbandry*.

After his death another edition of the book appeared which included some of his later articles on agriculture. It was translated into French and the Tullian system was adopted by several French landowners including Voltaire. He was an admirer of Tull's methods and used them on his estate at Ferney on the shores of Lake Geneva.

Towards the end of the 18th century English farmers looked more kindly on Tull's theories which were proving so popular on the Continent that they could no longer afford to ignore them.

In 1822 *Horse Hoing Husbandry*, with some alterations, was edited by William Cobbett of *Rural Rides* fame. His comment 'that book which does so much honour to his memory, and to whom the cultivators of England owe so much' epitomises the change of opinion which gradually overcame the prejudice originally attached to Tull's theories and inventions.

Jethro Tull, the gentleman farmer from London, had received due recognition at last.

Berkshire Charities

THROUGHOUT THE length and breadth of Berkshire men and women of every century have concerned themselves with the fate of those less fortunate than themselves. Before the advent of the Welfare State their thoughtfulness was especially welcome, indeed essential, if some measure of comfort was to be provided for the homeless, poor, and sick members of society.

In medieval times it was customary for wealthy men to endow almshouses for the aged poor who, in return, prayed for the well-being of their benefactors during their lifetime and for their souls in the life to come.

One such man owned lands in Estbury (now Eastbury) which was then part of the parish of Lambourn. John d'Estbury was granted a licence by Henry VII in 1501 to found a perpetual charity and almshouses for ten poor men. The following year the houses were built near the church of St Michael and All Angels in Lambourn. On the south side of the church a chapel was added and dedicated to the Holy Trinity. Here stands John d'Estbury's grey marble tomb around which the almsmen prayed. Their oak seats can still be seen and were used within living memory when the men came in their long cloaks to attend the daily service.

The almshouses were rebuilt by Henry Hippisley of Lambourn Place in 1852, and were modernised within recent years so that bathrooms could be provided for the almsmen. This necessitated a reduction in numbers from ten to eight but the improved facilities are appreciated by the residents.

A strange story is told of the founder's death. It is said that as he slept in his garden, apparently with his mouth wide open, a worm, or snake, popped in and resisted all the efforts of John's housekeeper to remove it. She thoughtfully provided a bowl of milk by way of persuasion but the intruder would not be tempted. Instead it repaid her efforts by stinging her master. A sting which caused his death.

The origin of the story is uncertain but it is considered that the strange text-bearing scroll which issues from the mouth of the brass figure on top of the founder's tomb may be indicative of the way he died. If it is so, it was a nasty end for so worthy a man.

At the opposite end of the county, in the Thameside village of Bray, there is another group of almshouses well known, not only for its own merit, which is considerable, but as the subject of Fred Walker's painting of 1872 entitled *The Harbour of Refuge*. It is an apt title for Jesus Hospital, which has provided a refuge for the elderly for over 350 years.

The founder, William Goddard, died in 1609. Under the terms of his will he 'devised to the wardens and commonalty of the mystery of Fishmongers of London, after the decease of his wife Joyce, lands in London and his lands in Bray, for the purpose of erecting almshouses to accommodate six aged and poor persons of the Company and thirty four aged and poor of the parish of Bray to be called Jesus Hospital in Bray of the foundation of William Goddard'.

Letters Patent were granted for the founding of the Hospital on 13th August 1616 but it was not until after the death of Joyce Goddard in 1622 that work was commenced on the group of forty almshouses, a chapel, and a chaplain's house over the entrance porch at the east end of the building. The work was completed between 1627 and 1628.

The houses stand round a quadrangle in the centre of which is the original pump from which the residents used to draw their water. No such primitive condition exists today. During

this century each group of three houses was made into two to enable kitchens and bathrooms to be provided for all the houses. The alterations reduced the number of course, and a further reduction will be made by current alterations whereby the original 'bedsitter' type of accommodation will be replaced by a separate living room and bedroom for every resident.

At one time each house had its own plot of garden within the quadrangle, but some residents were unable to manage the gardening. Therefore it was decided to make plots available at the back of the buildings for any who wanted them and to place the care of the quadrangle in the hands of a resident gardener. The result is a most beautiful garden which the residents can enjoy together, and passers-by can admire through the entrance archway.

Originally the services in the chapel were conducted by laymen, probably by some of the residents, but a chaplain was appointed in 1818 to care for the spiritual needs of the community while a resident matron is at hand to care for its material welfare.

Over the entrance porch stands the statue of the man who provided for the comfort of his fellow men and women – William Goddard, Merchant of London, and a free brother of the Fishmonger's Company.

Other similar foundations exist in the county but those who could not afford such munificence contented themselves by giving a little extra to the inhabitants of existing almshouses or to those who managed in their own homes on slender incomes.

Richard Dangerfield of Newbury bequeathed in his will of 20th January 1826, the sum of £400, the interest from which was to be divided between the almspeople of the Church almshouses, and the interest of a further £300 between the almspeople of Coxedd's and Pearce's almshouses. The latter charity favoured poor weavers to whom the decline in the woollen trade had brought great hardship. Noncomformists also benefiited from Richard Dangerfield's generosity for he left money to various societies of Protestant dissenters which was to be shared between their poorer members.

Barbara Jordan thought of those women who were left to battle on alone, probably after a lifetime of service to elderly parents or relatives. In 1730 she left money to be distributed to three ancient maidens on St Thomas's Day. She directed that they must have been born, and still reside, in New Windsor.

Some charities were bestowed in kind rather than in money. The Rev. Martin Annesley, an 18th century rector of Frilsham and vicar of Bucklebury, left implicit instructions about the way in which his funeral was to be conducted. There were to be no undertakers or pallbearers and the money thus saved was to be spent on the provision of sixpenny loaves to the poor people of his two parishes.

Reed's charity of Hampstead Norreys provided a blue greatcoat yearly for a man of good character who had worked on one farm for at least ten years. This gift was continued into this century. The *Newbury Weekly News* reported in 1908 that Daniel Butler was the recipient of the coat in that year. He worked at Eling Farm. The gift was considered to be a 'badge of honour' — a reward for long and good service.

Many bequests have been made for the benefit of apprentice boys but Archbishop Laud, a native of Reading, also remembered the maidservants when he gave by deed dated 26th March 1640 to the Corporation of Reading certain lands so that money could be paid every two years for the apprenticeship of twelve young boys, with preference to the fatherless, and every third year in gifts to six poor maidens for their marriage portions, both boys and maids to be born in Reading, Wokingham or Bray.

Other Reading gentlemen followed the lead of the Archbishop. Firstly, John Blagrave in 1611, and later three others who chose a novel way of selecting the recipients of their charity.

In 1755 William Boudry and John Richards left land, the rents from which were to pay 4s.0d. to the Clerk who administered the charity, 1s.0d. to the bellman, who presumably summoned the maidens to apply, and the residue was for the lucky winner. She was to be one of three maidservants chosen from the three parishes of Reading. All applicants were to be members of the established church who should have served in a household of good name and fame for at least five years within one of the said parishes. When the finalists had been chosen they were assembled together and required to throw dice to decide the winner. It is to be hoped that her feet were not then set on a gambler's path for ever!

In 1809, Martin Annesley, the son of the benevolent rector,

and the M.P. for Reading for thirty years, must have felt sorry for the two unlucky maidservants. He made a gift of £300 consuls, increased to £500 in 1820, to provide gifts of £4 and £3 to the unsuccessful finalists.

The throwing of dice evidently caused displeasure to the Victorian administrators of the charity for that practice was discontinued in 1861 when the charities of Blagrave, Boundry, Richards, and Annesley were amalgamated to become The Consolidated Charities for Female Servants at Reading. It continued as such until the lack of suitable applicants caused the terms of the charity to be changed so that the money could be distributed to students instead of the non-existent maid-servants.

Education has not been forgotten. Long before state education was introduced the Church and private benefactors provided schooling for some fortunate children. Frequently clothing was supplied as well, and Blue Coat and Green Coat schools were especially popular both in towns and villages.

The aunt of the lord of the manor of Bucklebury wept with joy when she saw the children of his Green Coat school wear their new clothes on Easter Day, 1816. Six poor boys and six poor girls attended the school to learn reading, writing, arithmetic and the catechism from a teacher who was paid twelve pounds a year in addition to being allowed a free house and her heating. She taught the girls needlework while the boys learned a trade. Although the school was absorbed into the national school later in the century the twelve selected children continued to wear the distinctive uniform until early this century when the expense of the clothing, coupled with the fact that twentieth century children no longer wished to wear the outmoded dress, made it expedient to replace the gift of clothes by that of vouchers which could be spent at a Newbury store. The recipients of the charity no longer stood apart from their more fortunate schoolmates.

Perhaps the most famous of the county's Blue Coat schools is the one founded in Reading in 1646 by Richard Aldworth, Merchant of London and Reading, and a Governor of Christ's

Hospital. No doubt inspired by that famous foundation, he started a school for twenty poor boys in Reading on a site at the corner of Silver Street and London Road. Further benefactions were made which enabled the school to be expanded and thirty six boys were receiving education by 1720. This caused severe overcrowding and the original school was demolished and another was built on the same site, but this became inadequate by 1853 and a move was made to larger premises in the Bath Road.

In this century the site could no longer provide the necessary facilities needed by a flourishing independent school. It was moved out of Reading to Holme Park, Sonning, in 1947. Nearly 500 scholars, boarders and day-boys, now attend the school. The boarders still wear the traditional gowns and yellow stockings on special occasions. Richard Aldworth would be proud to see them – a success story which had such humble beginnings 340 years ago.

Cippenham's Royal Marriage

A S ONE STANDS on the bridge over the M4 motorway at Cippenham the past and the present are brought vividly together by the surrounding scene.

New housing estates and industrial buildings stand beyond the hedgerows. Below, a continuous stream of traffic divides the fields which once formed part of the medieval domain of Richard, Earl of Cornwall, second son of King John and brother to Henry III. Nearby the remains of an ancient moat is thought to mark the site where his castle stood in the midst of his deer park. It was to this castle that the young earl brought his bride, Isabella, in the spring of 1231.

It was in some respects a remarkable match. Richard was 22 years old. The bride was nine years his senior, the widow of Gilbert de Clere, Earl of Gloucester, to whom she had borne six children in their sixteen years of marriage. Isabella had married de Clere when she was only fourteen years of age, and was widowed when he died in Brittany in 1230 while campaigning with Henry III and Richard of Cornwall. The earl's body was taken to Tewkesbury Abbey for burial and the bereaved countess remained there under the protection of the Abbot.

Isabella de Clere was a renowned noblewoman. Not only was she the widow of the Earl of Gloucester but she was also the third daughter of the late William the Marshall, Earl of Pembroke. Of all his ten children, five sons and five daughters, she was held to be the one who most resembled her father, having inherited in good measure his bravery, ability, and charm of manner. William had proved himself even as a child when his father, John Marshall, had sent him as a hostage to King Stephen during the siege of Newbury Castle in 1152. Twice John Marshall placed his son's life in jeopardy when he failed to comply with the agreed terms thereby arousing the justifiable anger of the king who threatened the boy with certain death. On both occasions the boy's outstanding courage and personal charm stayed the king's hand. Not only did Stephen spare the child's life but he chose to amuse his young hostage. In turn they plucked the flowers from a plant, probably the common plantain, as they played the old game of Soldiers or Speargrass.

As William grew to manhood he was destined for high honours throughout his long life. A gallant soldier and wise statesman he served England well, and as a revered elder statesman, William the Marshall, Earl of Pembroke, lord of Striguil (Chepstow) and lord of Leinster, became Regent of England during the early years of Henry III's minority. The whole country mourned his passing when he died in 1219, in his eightieth year, at his manor of Caversham, surrounded by his family, church dignitaries, and statesmen. The Earl was succeeded by his eldest son, another William, who married Eleanor, daughter of King John, and sister to Henry III and the Earl of Cornwall. It was to William Marshall the younger, his brother-in-law, that Richard turned for permission to marry the beautiful Isabella.

The matter was one of urgency. King Henry had spoken of finding a suitable bride for his younger brother, but Richard had no wish to marry a woman of his brother's choosing purely for political reasons. He had seen Isabella and had fallen deeply in love with her. The Earl was convinced that no other woman would make him happy. He rode in haste to Striguil where William Marshall was staying in the early part of 1231 and laid his proposal before him. William gladly gave his consent and promised to help. Both men knew that they would incur the King's displeasure when they decided to keep the marriage secret until it was safely accomplished rather than risk any interference from Henry.

Richard left Striguil to make his way to Tewkesbury where he found Isabella and soon persuaded her to accept his proposal. She then travelled to her brother's castle at Caversham and in due course the marriage party proceeded to Fawley, another Thames-side manor of the Earl Marshall. There the wedding took place on the 13th March 1231.

The young earl lost no time in taking his bride to his castle at Cippenham but it was not a great stronghold and they must have waited in some trepidation for news of the reaction of the King when he learned of the secret and hasty union of his brother and heir to the throne. No doubt the earl and his new countess were poised for flight and may well have been forced to seek a safer refuge than Cippenham's wooden castle but for the Countess of Pembroke who acted as peacemaker between her two brothers.

At length the King accepted the defeat of his own plan for Richard's future and sent for the newly-wed pair to attend him at Windsor. They must have travelled to the fortress with some misgivings but they were well received by Henry and Isabella's beauty and ability soon found favour in the eyes of her royal brother-in-law.

One month after the marriage, on the 13th April, the King presided at a banquet which he gave in honour of the occasion and was particularly gracious and courteous to the bride. She had indeed inherited the good qualities of her father and once again the courage and charm of a Marshall succeeded in calming the anger of a king.

The Castle Inn Scandal

THE MEETING and dinner of the Colnbrook Turnpike Commissioners which was held at the Castle Inn, Salthill, on March 29th 1773, not only brought illness and death in its wake but also an aftermath of deception, misplaced loyalties, and false accusations, which all added furore to the mystery surrounding the tragic event.

At first the news of what was happening to the Commissioners was sketchy as though the principals in the drama were loathe to admit the seriousness of the affair, but as the days passed and the death-toll mounted the county and London newspapers took up the story of that fateful day.

The *Berkshire Chronicle* published a full report of the proceedings on the 26th April 1773. The names of the gentlemen who were present at the meeting were given as follows: Honourable Mr. O'Brien, Mr. Needham, Edward Mason, Major Mayne, – Cheshire, Walpole Eyre, Esq., Captain Salter, Mr. Isherwood, Mr. Benwell, treasurer, Mr. Pote sen. and Burcombe, the surveyor.

The dinner, which was described as 'plain and innocent', offered a surprisingly wide range of food, namely: turtle soup, fish, jack, perch and eel spitch-cocket, fowls, bacon and greens, veal cutlets, ragout of pig's ears, chine of mutton and salad, course of lamb and cucumber, crayfish, pastry, and jellies.

Within a short time, (and this period of time was not clearly defined) nearly all the gentlemen were taken ill and in the cases of Captain Needham, Mr. Eyre, Mr. Isherwood, Mr. Benwell and Mr. Burcombe the illness proved fatal. Major Mayne was still dangerously ill.

Naturally, the first suspicions were cast on the food and drink that had been consumed at the dinner, but the landlady of the Castle Inn, a Mrs. Partridge opened her kitchen and cellar for inspection. It was stressed that nothing was highly seasoned, and nothing could give cause for suspicion or any bad consequences. The wine, madeira, and port, were of a good quality, and the company had not eaten or drunk to excess. So it was considered that no blame could be attached to the meal. Rather, it was thought, the illness could be attributed to the condition of a pauper who was brought to the inn with other poor people for examination by the magistrates.

It was the custom of those days to return the poor to their own parishes if possible so that the liability for their upkeep should not fall upon a parish in which they had taken up temporary residence. As some of the Commissioners were also Justices of the Peace it had seemed convenient to hold a meeting on the same morning as the Turnpike meeting to decide the fate of these poor souls. All the gentlemen remained in the room apart from Mr. Pote, a printer from Eton, who had attended the Commissioners on business but left the room to take a stroll in the garden during the magisterial meeting. He was the only one who was not taken ill although he later dined with the Commissioners.

Dr. James, who was attending the seriously ill Major Mayne, was of the opinion that his illness, and that of the deceased, had been caused by infection and not occasioned by anything they had eaten or drunk as the first symptoms did not occur until eleven days after the meeting whereas an illness of a poisonous nature would have occurred within hours of taking the poison.

In support of this theory it was said that one of the deceased, Mr. Burcombe, the surveyor, had not dined with the Commissioners but had eaten beefsteaks below stairs.

Regarding the wine, it was pointed out that the gentlemen drank of the same wine which they had commended at their former meetings, and which many had drank before and since the occasion.

So it appeared that the blame was upon the distressed pauper, or, and this was another possibility, upon some felons who were being transferred from Reading Gaol to London for transportation. It so happened that these poor wretches had stopped at the Inn that morning and it was suggested that one of them could have been suffering from gaol fever. Rumours were rife and heated discussions took place as to the cause of the tragedy.

Mrs. Partridge must have been relieved that these alternative suggestions countered speculation about the quality of the fare she offered to her customers but the matter was not to rest so easily. As the *Chronicle* reported on May 7th 1773, 'the late unhappy affair at Salt Hill has made a great noise through every part of the country'. It was to continue to do so for some time in spite of a letter which was sent to Mrs. Partridge by Dr. James and Dr. Huck that they were in agreement that the disease was of a contagious nature.

This opinion was confirmed by a Dr. Hugh Kennedy, who was called upon to attend Captain O'Brien. He asserted that he had had considerable experience in the treatment of gaol fever, both in this country and abroad, and he was convinced that his patient was suffering from a putrid disorder which he was treating with success. Dr. Kennedy was also convinced that it was caught from the pauper whom, he had been told, could not stand without support.

However, a 'Wellwisher to the Public', as a correspondent from Windsor styled himself, was not so sure the pauper was to blame. He asserted that reports published to the effect that the illness was caused by a contagious disease (and Mr. Pote of Eton had circulated handbills in support of this theory) were extremely suspect. He accused the propagators of such theories of spreading them for their own interests and to the detriment of the town of Windsor.

In support of his accusations he added that a report that the sympton did not appear till Good Friday, eleven days after the meeting 'is untrue for it is known that Mr. Isherwood was given over before that time, and the whole company were taken ill the very night following the dinner which is a fact known to everyone, whatever Dr. James, or somebody for him may assert. Again Mr. Burcombe, the surveyor, who ate his beefsteak below, is no proof that the wine he drank above stairs did not affect him in the manner which has since brought him to the grave but, on the contrary, the strongest. argument for it'.

'Wellwisher' also argued, with good reason, that if the paupers had passed on the disease to the Commissioners, why had none of the servants below caught it, likewise the people where the poor wretches had lodged? He considered that Mrs. Partridge should endeavour to trace the vagrants, especially the extremely distressed one, to confirm or deny these queries.

The anonymous correspondent had obviously made inquiries about the condition of the Commissioners who had survived the ordeal. Captain O'Brien was still not quite out of danger. Captain Salter, who had been taken ill immediately upon returning home, and drunk warm salt water which had made him vomit. Mr. Mason was then under a course of salt water drinking which produced the same effect. Mr. Williams (who was not mentioned in the original list) went to Chichester directly after the dinner. He developed a high fever and called a physician who cared for him properly so that he recovered. Mr. Cheshire had dosed himself with strong physic as soon as he felt unwell with apparent success. A final comment: 'How Mr. Pote escaped is hard to account for unless the soup which he ate before dinner could fortify his stomach.'

The report continued, 'Had the disease been contagious all or some of those who attended the disease must have been affected but nothing like that had appeared, though Dr. James perhaps insured their lives as he had endeavoured to insure the reputation of Mrs. Partridge's house by injudiciously opposing his physical reasoning to known facts and all for what? For supporting an individual at the expense of the quiet of the country; by this means setting a mark upon Windsor as an affected place, deterring strangers and injuring the inhabitants, when at this time there was no more wholesome place in Europe.'

After these scathing comments 'Wellwisher' came to the conclusion that the wine had been tainted as several of the company had noticed a remarkable taste. He blamed the refiners of the wine and added that Mrs. Partiridge was to be pitied but for the public good it would be better if the truth was told rather than a tale of contagion which only scared the public.

Mrs. Partridge promptly replied that she had indeed traced the history of the distressed pauper. On April 30th she had sent a letter to the *Gazetteer* affirming that James Jackson, a poor fellow, was found ill in the stables of a Mr. March at Taplow. He was carried into the house and nursed by the wife of one Matthews. She was taken ill of a fever but had recovered, but her husband had caught it and since died. Mrs. Partridge added that the Rev. Mr. Hamilton of Taplow, and a Mr. Newberry, would confirm this story.

James Jackson was then brought by cart by the parish officer to the Castle Inn on the 29th March and the Gentlemen had ordered his removal to Wooburn. The poor man was taken by cart to an outhouse at the Royal Oak. Within ten days, Mrs. Partridge asserted, the woman who carried food to Jackson was seized of a fever and died and the barber who shaved him was dangerously ill. It seemed that the Castle Inn landlady was on the way of successfully proving her innocence in the affair, but not for long.

On May 28th the *Berkshire Chronicle* printed 'Further particulars relative to Salthill' which not only included more theories about possible additions of various agents, including arsenic, in the refining of wine but also replied to Mrs. Partridge's account of James Jackson's activities. It was stated that the pauper was not suffering from any contagious disease but the effects of lack of food and clothing, that the woman

89

who had cared for him at Taplow was very well, and that her husband who had died had been ill for nine years. None of the March family who had helped him in his distress had suffered from any ill effects. Furthermore, the woman who had carried food to him at Wooburn was very old and very ill before she came into contact with him, and there were no cases of infectious disease in the county.

A final shaft at Mrs. Partridge was the observation that none of her servants, who were numerous, had caught the infection although they had come into contact with the pauper.

Having presented all known facts and correspondence regarding the case without solving the mystery, the press allowed the matter to rest. No doubt, it was discussed for months around the county whenever people met together for business or pleasure. It says much for Mrs. Partridge's reputation that many were ready to defend her and continued to use the Castle Inn. As in the past the Commissioners of the Colnbrook Turnpike Trust alternated the venue for their meetings between the Castle and Windmill Inns.

They might not have been so trusting had they but known the truth. It was finally revealed in the *Memoirs of Charlotte Papendick*, who was the assistant keeper of the wardrobe to Queen Charlotte and lived at Windsor. (*The Great Bath Road* by Daphne Phillips). Apparently Mrs. Partridge confessed on her deathbed that the turtle soup was the cause of the disaster. It had been left overnight in a copper pan, the bottom of which had become green with verdi gris. When the soup was reheated in the morning the existing poison had become aggravated by the addition of acid flavourings. For years Mrs. Partridge had kept her awful secret, plagued, no doubt, by her conscience which finally made her confess her guilt. To her credit she stated that the cook was unaware of the danger and was in no way to blame for the accident.

It came to light also that Mr. Burcombe, the surveyor, had not eaten beefsteak below stairs as had been originally claimed, but had dined from the remains of the upstairs meal.

That accounted for his unfortunate demise but what of Mr. Pote's miraculous escape from harm?

Could the clue to his good fortune be in 'Wellwisher's' comment, 'unless the soup which he ate before dinner could fortify his stomach?' Obviously, this soup could not have been of the turtle variety which was served to the gentlemen. Perhaps another had been prepared for general consumption and, after his stroll in the garden, Mr. Pote had taken a bowl of this variety *before* dinner as stated by 'Wellwisher', with the result that he refused the turtle soup when he sat down to dine. If this supposition is correct it could explain why Mr. Pote alone suffered no sickness amongst those who dined at the Castle Inn on that ill-fated March day in 1773.

Mary Russell Mitford

THE COTTAGE in Three Mile Cross where Mary Russell Mitford lived for thirty years has been converted into offices, and the tree lined turnpike road between Reading and Basingstoke now vibrates to the roar of twentieth century traffic, but beyond the village lie the fields, the woods, and the lanes where Miss Mitford once walked with Mayflower, her beloved greyhound. Occasionally she would stop to exchange greetings with her friends. There was shy Hannah, destined to marry the son of a wealthy hatter of Reading, the industrious, pale, and sickly looking shoemaker, Joe Kirby the young cricketer, or Lizzie, the seven year old daughter of the village carpenter. All these, and many more, she introduced into the pages of her famous book *Our Village*.

The authoress was not a native of Berkshire. She was born in Alresford, Hampshire, on 16th December 1787, the only surviving child of Dr. George Mitford and his wife, Mary. The doctor was not a busy country practitioner as one might suppose, but a gentleman of leisure. He had married an heiress, ten years his senior, and was quite content to live on her income and indulge his passion for gambling. Fortune did not always smile upon him. During Mary's childhood the family moved to Reading, Lyme Regis, and finally to London, by which time his wife's fortune was so depleted that George Mitford was in serious financial difficulties, but he still retained the gambler's optimistic hope that his luck must change.

Mary's tenth birthday was at hand so the doctor took the child to purchase her present – a lottery ticket! She was allowed to choose the number and immediately selected 2224. The lottery office keeper shook his head. Part of that ticket was already sold. Mary was told to choose another number but she was adamant. It must be 2224 as the total of those numbers represented the years of her age. The keeper probably thought her a precocious and troublesome child, but her father regarded her insistence as a propitious omen. He bought out the part owner of the ticket and Mary had her present. For once, Dr. Mitford's intuition did not fail him. Ticket number 2224 won a prize of £20,000.

Having disposed of his wife's money George Mitford now lost no time in spending that of his daughter. He purchased a house in London Road, Reading. Here he became friendly with M. St. Quintin, a French refugee, who wife taught at the Abbey School. Later the St Quintins opened a school in London at 22 Hans Place where Mary was sent as a boarder in 1798. It was probably the best thing that Dr. Mitford ever did for her. By 18th century standards she received a good education and returned home in 1802 an accomplished young lady with a taste for literature.

Mary Mitford's first published work *Miscellaneous Poems* appeared in 1810 and further volumes of poetry found favour both in this country and in America. She visited London frequently, moved in literary circles, and made influential friends. These included Samuel Coleridge who encouraged her to write tragic poetical works.

It was providential that she was so talented. By 1820 her father had once more reduced his family to penury after buying and lavishly rebuilding a farmhouse in Grazely where he, his wife, and daughter, enjoyed an elegant life style until mounting debts forced them to leave their home. They found refuge in a labourer's cottage which was situated between the village inn and a general shop in Three Mile Cross. After the

spaciousness of Bertram House, their Grazely home, the cramped conditions of the cottage must have been almost unbearable. The largest room was eight feet square. With her customary resilience to misfortune Mary proceeded to plant the garden with her favourite flowers in an endeavour to brighten the mean surroundings of her new home.

Now her writing was the only means of support for the family. Apparently it did not occur to Dr. Mitford that he should exert himself to improve his income. In her own words, Mary Russell Mitford descended 'from the lofty steep of tragic poetry to the every day path of village stories'. It was to prove a path paved with success.

The first sketches of village life appeared in the *Lady's Magazine* in 1819. The sales of the periodical rose sharply as readers clamoured for more news from 'Our Village'. They eagerly awaited the stories of the village cricket matches, the day to day events in the lives of the villagers, the descriptions of the wild creatures and the hedgerow flowers so vividly portrayed by the authoress.

Early stories were published in one volume in 1824. It was the first of many, so popular have the tales remained to this day.

Not that poetry and plays were altogether neglected. Mary Mitford also enjoyed success as a playright. *Julian* (1823) and *Foscari* were both produced at Covent Garden and *Rienzi* (1828) at Drury Lane Theatre. This play, a poetical tragedy was considered her best work for the theatre. It ran for thirty four performances and eight thousand copies were sold.

In November 1829 *Foscari* and *Rienzi* were produced by Edward Barnett at Reading Theatre. In both plays the lead was taken by Mr. Cathcart whose acting ability was held in high esteem by Miss Mitford. She attended the theatre regularly to write reviews of Mr. Barnett's presentations for the *Reading Mercury*.

Mary's mother died in 1830 leaving Mary to provide and care for her wayward father. A thankless task indeed. Not only did he squander his daughter's money but he made demands upon her time by asking her to read aloud to him and to bear him company. He hated to be alone and resented her absence if she visited her friends. In spite of all hindrances the plays, poems, reviews, and contributions to various magazines, flowed from her pen. Another major work *Belford Regis*, or *Sketches of a Country Town* appeared in 1835 and her Berkshire readers had no difficulty in recognizing Reading as the subject of this book. It enjoyed considerable success although it lacked the spontaneous charm of *Our Village*. Elizabeth Barrett (afterwards Mrs. Browning) thought well of it and was able to convey her personal congratulations to the authoress when the two ladies were introduced to each other in 1836 on one of Miss Mitford's now rare visits to London. They became firm friends and corresponded frequently. The grant of a civil pension of £100 a year made in 1837 helped alleviate financial pressure, at least for a time, and later that year alterations were made to the cottage at Three Mile Cross. Miss Mitford wrote to tell her new friend about 'a pretty upstairs sitting room, 13ft. square, with a little ante-room lined with books, both looking on to the garden'. At last she could write in comparative comfort.

Unfortunately, her financial troubles were by no means at an end. Early in 1842 Mary admitted that she had not bought a gown, cloak, bonnet, or hardly a pair of new gloves for four years, but she never once criticized or blamed her spendthrift father. He died later that year, on December 11th, and left a pile of debts to be settled by his long-suffering daughter. The bills were paid by public subscription and the surplus that remained helped to boost Mary's scanty savings.

Her health began to deteriorate but her spirit remained undaunted. Her great friend, the Rev. Charles Kingsley, rode over from his parish of Eversley to see her and other friends travelled from London to the little cottage where she continued to live until 1851. Then she decided to move nearer to her friend Lady Russell of Swallowfield Park.

It is said that Mary Mitford's beloved books were packed on a hand cart and pushed along the lanes to her new home. This story was verified a few years ago by an old lady who recalled that her grandfather had seen the occurrence when he was a boy in Swallowfield. Unfortunately, shortly after her move, a carriage accident while she was being driven through Swallowfield Park caused severe injuries and she became confined to the house.

In 1852 *Recollections of a Literary Life* was published, and two years later, *Atherton and other Tales*. This book was highly praised by Mr. Ruskin and it was to be her last. Mary Russell Mitford died on 10th January 1855. By her own request she was buried in Swallowfield Churchyard and not, as her friends had expected, at Shinfield Church where her parents were buried, near the village of Three Mile Cross.

Perhaps she chose wisely. The quiet corner where a granite cross marks her resting place remains unchanged. The nearby footpath still leads across Swallowfield Park, and the great house, now divided into elegant flats, retains the grandeur of more gracious days when Lady Russell sent her carriage to fetch Miss Mitford for afternoon tea.